D1526892

I'll Never Walk Alone
by
Maria Anne Hirschmann

Hansi Books
Fallbrook, California 92028

© Copyright 1986 by Maria Anne Hirschmann
Hansi Ministries, Inc.
Fallbrook, CA 92028

Published by Hansi Ministries, Inc.
Fallbrook, CA 92028
All rights reserved
Printed in U.S.A.

Library of Congress Catalog Card No. 78-58744
ISBN-0-932878-08-3

Foreword

The church was already crowded! I had arrived about five minutes before the meeting was to start and I had to search for a place to sit. "She must be good," I thought. We had all come to hear a lady speak who loved the Lord Jesus and the country He had given her for her new homeland, America.

The lady was Hansi and I listened and was thrilled with the new insights about freedom that she gave me. "She *is* a good speaker," I admitted to myself. "She's the sort of person I wish I knew," I decided. Little did I realize that the Lord had it all in His plan and someday we would work together and serve Him all over the world.

In His timing He brought it all about. I joined Hansi Ministries and the Lord began to teach us so many new things. This book is written to share these and many other ideas with you. As Hansi wrote and the story of God's rebuilding of a life and a life-work unfolded, the all-sufficiency of Jesus as Lord and Husband to a lonely lady unfolded, too.

"How much of your story may I tell?" she asked me one day.

"Tell whatever you and the Lord feel would be helpful," I answered her. "After all He is my Lord and Husband, too. The only difference is that He is the only husband I've ever had."

This is our story. Or, to be more exact, this is the story of how Jesus works in the lives of two people who more than anything else want to let Him be in charge of everything: spirit, soul and body. I am honored to be included in the story.

Betty Pershing
Fallbrook, CA
May 1986

New Year's Day/*Sunday*

The dark leafless arms of the big tree in front of my bedroom window were outlined against the pale rosy glow of dawn. Branches softly scraped and knocked against the glass as the gentle ocean breeze wafted over them.

I woke up and knew the rain had stopped. It would be a sunny day, the kind of California weather I loved —cool and bright. It was early, too early to get up and disturb the other sleepers in the house. I didn't want to get up anyway, I just wanted to lie very still and experience the great change within myself.

The moment I opened my eyes this morning I knew that life had taken a turn. It took me a few moments to figure out why I felt so different. My heavy burden had vanished, leaving me with a sensation of freedom, joy, and puzzlement. How could the world change so drastically in twenty-four hours? Outwardly nothing has changed, either for the better or worse.

I am still the same divorced woman I have been for the past few long years; my financial situation is still tight and unpredictable; so is the behavior of my five children. Sometimes they love me, other times they reject and blame me for our broken home and any other growing pains they experience. I lease a four–bedroom house near the beach but, since I resigned from my position as a teacher, I am seldom around. I travel most of the year, reserving the holidays for my family and myself. I cherish every precious minute I can be home.

Peter is sleeping downstairs in his waterbed. Most likely one or more of his high school chums are snoring in sleeping bags on the carpet of his room, or even in the living room, and I will have to step over them to get to the kitchen. I heard several voices when my son returned from a New Year's Eve party at his girl friend's house long after midnight.

In the room next to mine sleeps Betty, my associate in the ministry. We decided to make the upstairs the ladies' domain. The downstairs belongs to the men of the house, mainly Peter, my youngest son, and his schoolmates, and to Tim whenever he decides to stay overnight. Tim is my oldest boy and lives in an apartment near his college. He is only a few driving hours away. Tina, my oldest daughter, and her husband live on the other side of the country. Kathy and Heidi are together at the same college, but it takes a day's drive for them to come and see me. So, if anyone asks me, I say that I would have to say I am more or less alone.

Yes, *I am alone*. But that is the new difference I feel within me: I am as alone as I was before but not *lonely* anymore. Gone are my feelings of being forsaken, misunderstood, and ostracized by society. I am no longer a prisoner on a deserted island—when I think of the many difficulties, agonies, heartbreaks, sleepless nights, confused and lonely times I have experienced during the last few years!

Ever since the divorce became final I wondered if I should chase rainbows and eligible men or bury myself away in a remote mountain cabin. I had even suggested to the Lord that I could buy a one-way ticket to Europe and vanish.

Suddenly the conflict is over! What has happened? Until today I never knew what *one* resolute straight forward decision could do for a life — my life. I would not have dared to wish or hope for as much peace and joy as I feel right now. What a day! What a way to begin a new year! And I could have missed it by merely refusing to make a clear-cut, hard decision.

This past year the hint of romance, a great new love, and the possibility of a second marriage had tiptoed into my life. It left me dreaming and also searching for God's perfect will. "Lord, what is Your wish in this matter?" I prayed over and over. "I am Your hand-maiden. You called me into a ministry mainly to the evangelical churches of America. The churches are divided on the issue of divorce and remarriage. I don't know where the true answer lies, but You do, Lord. I want to do Your will first; please show me which way to walk and I will obey."

"You may go either way," the Lord seemed to answer repeatedly and always so very tenderly. "Whatever you decide, I shall bless you and use you. Remember that I gave you this new friendship. But you won't disobey Me if you do not wish to pursue it."

I thought about it. I pleaded, cried, and argued with God to please tell me what to do and I would follow His orders willingly. But I knew deep within my heart that the final decision was mine to make, and it frightened me. Jesus had never dealt like this with me before. I was used to His clear-cut marching orders in my life. All my choices had consisted only of deciding between right and wrong. For the first time in my Christian experience I had to choose between two rights. But even if both pathways led to the same good end, there had to be one that was better than the other. One way had to be God's *perfect* will, and I sensed a growing conviction about it.

In long sleepless night hours and through dazed daytime activities I battled my fears of being alone. I struggled with financial concerns, wondered if my son needed male companionship more than just inadequate me, and fought thousands of other worries. The future looked like a dark tunnel of isolation and loneliness and I could see no light at the end of the tunnel. I don't think I ever battled a deeper depression in all my life, and I have had countless severe depression attacks in my stormy past. Then, last night, New Year's Eve, I drove up to the mountains. I sat on a big rock under a few stars and the Lord and I talked.

"Jesus," I said, "I thank You for the beautiful choice You gave me. It did so much for me. But You know my final decision. I need nobody but You. You are sufficient. All I want to do is serve You. Remember, Lord, what I said in the women's retreat last month? I ended the message by saying that I knew I was a crushed leaf, the kind we used to lay on wounds for healing in my childhood. If I married I might become a whole leaf again, someone who would be accepted by most of society as 'normal.' But I'd rather stay crushed, Lord. I'd rather stay with You alone, Jesus."

I drove down the mountain road in deep darkness, the stars hidden behind clouds. I sensed the presence of Jesus in a new way. He seemed to hold all of me, my tired body, my weary soul, the whole lonely me. When I finally tiptoed into my bedroom, I fell asleep in His arms.

This early morning I woke up, and I am free!

End of January/
Wednesday Night

My sense of newfound joy and freedom has stayed with me since Near Year's Day. I wondered if it would, or if I had been blessed by an unexpected "emotional high" for a single day. It is not a physical or emotional experience, I found out, because I still get my morning headaches, and my ever-ready tears spill over as usual.

The Lord has helped me to sort things out. Not that I have gotten the whole puzzle figured out yet, but I sense a clear new direction. For the first time I also see a light at the end of my tunnel. The Lord and I have been talking a lot lately. I am so thankful that my January schedule was not as heavy as usual. Jesus knew I would need some quiet hours to think and talk it all through with Him. He is so very good to me. I get overwhelmed by His willingness to help me with even the smallest details of daily living, and not only the big issues of my broken home and life.

I shall never forget this last New Year's Day. It not only gave me a new closeness with the Lord but also the beginning of a precious human friendship I did not expect.

When I finally got up that New Year's Day morning Betty had long since left to teach a Bible class. I put on my grubbies, went downstairs, climbed over some still snoring teenage boys and slipped out through the sliding glass door to the backyard. I love to work with the soil, even if it is just pulling weeds. God is nearest when I am around flowers and trees. (Weeding also puts me in a kneeling position, which is not only humbling but necessary for my aching back.)

In the bright sunshine of a new day I poured my heart

out in silent thanksgiving. "Lord," I said, "it is like I walked out of a nightmare into the morning sun. I feel warm and good and at peace and I thank You. I don't understand why, but I don't have to understand it all before I can praise You, do I?"

Through the "still small voice" within me the Lord answered back, and I know His voice by now because Jesus and I have been friends for many years. He said, "You made a clear decision for Me, My Child, and Satan tried to hinder and scare you. But when you resist the devil he has to flee. He cannot always bother you. I will not permit it. Right now you are in the glow of victory."

"Lord," I said and watched a butterfly swing from flower to flower, "I did not expect to ever feel so happy and light as I do right now. I thank You, and You know my heart, I didn't make my decision for that reason. I just wanted to serve You no matter what. And I thought it meant sadness and loneliness for the rest of my life."

"I know your heart," the Lord interrupted me tenderly, "but why do you think I would find pleasure in your loneliness — or in any of My children's despair? Am I not a God of love? So you were willing to be lonely for My sake — and *you shall never walk alone again!*"

My tears began to roll when I answered Him: "Thank You, my Lord, I know that You will never leave me nor forsake me and that is enough for me!"

"I will be with you always," the Lord said and then He continued to tell me that He had more for me than just His presence through the Holy Spirit. "It is not good for you to be humanly alone and I have companionship for you that will be better than the marriage you just lost," the Lord said to me.

I heard what He said but it did not make sense to me. I had just chosen to be alone and now He told me that it wasn't good for me? "Lord," I prayed, "I do not need to remind You where I come from. I am that little orphan girl who grew up in a remote mountain village in the heart of Europe and slept in a hayloft. I am still Your dumb kid and I don't seem to be able to grasp Your kind

words. What do You mean by 'companionship'? I have
the children and many friends. Isn't it enough? Also,
what could be better than marriage?"

"Marriage is My very special gift to the human race,
but I have one gift that surpasses it: Friendship. And
the love of friends can be deeper and greater than some
marriage ties," the Lord spoke clearly.

I stood up and wiped my eyes with my sleeve. I looked
up into the blue sky and said aloud: "Jesus, I have asked
You for this often lately, but right now I must ask for it
again in a very special way. Whatever I understood You
to say, will You please verify it for me right from the
Bible? I have to know for sure that You are talking to
me. Nobody will believe what You just said, especially
in America where people look at marriage as the
ultimate fulfillment. Even single people like Betty come
under attack and she certainly does not deserve it. She
has served You faithfully all her life, and she loves You
and she is one fine lady, I know that for sure."

"Go to your Bible," the Lord nudged me kindly, "and
find the chapters that tell about David and Jonathan."

I went inside, washed my hands, picked up my
German Bible and found the story in the books of
Samuel. Scanning the familiar narrative I found two
verses I had never noticed before: David describes his
friendship with Jonathan as more precious than his
love for his wives. Next the Bible makes it clear that
God Himself "knit their souls together" in a special
bond of friendship. I wondered why I had not seen these
things before.

"I have given you and Betty the same gift of friendship," the Lord said as I meditated over the Bible story.
"I have put you together. People can be put together by
my Spirit in different ways: in marriage, as families, as
partners for My work — and as friends. I gave you the
best I have to give."

It boggled my mind that someone so special as Betty
might become my best friend, and for always. I couldn't
think of anything better. She had come to work for our

young ministry more than a year ago. In order to join us she resigned from a secure position as a senior editor in a well-known Christian publishing company. She gave up all her earthly securities, including retirement bene-fits, when she joined the ministry. But she went one step further and gave up the independence and privacy she was used to as a single person when she agreed to move into my home to help us out. My secretary who had lived with us had found her own apartment.

I did not want Peter to stay by himself in this big house. The arrangement had worked out extremely well for the last year, but sometimes I wondered if Betty hadn't sacrificed too much in the process. Sure, my children loved her and I found her an easygoing, pleasant and very unusual person. Her knowledge of the Bible and the Hebrew culture seemed to be a never-ending resource and inspiration to me.

In my intense emotional struggle for the last few months I had not given any other friendship too much thought except one — and now that was over! After my decision I had braced myself for a lone walk with God, and now I heard the Lord saying: "I had everything planned for you all along, you were just too preoccupied to see it." I wondered what Betty would have to say about it.

When she returned from church she walked into the kitchen in her pleasant smiling way and I said serious-ly: "I have to share something with you. While you were gone the Lord showed me something special." I picked up my Bible and read to her the David and Jonathan story. Then I said, "Jesus told me He has this kind of friendship for you and me. Did you know that?" I didn't hesitate to talk to her in my own "peculiar" vocabulary because she talks with the Lord the same way I do and understands what I mean. I wondered if God had told her already.

Obviously He had not! Betty looked at me with a puzzled expression and did not answer. "Look, Betty," I hastened to explain, "I can understand if it would bother you. I am fully aware that you take the greater risk. People will gossip about you as they have about me. Your reputation is impeccable, you have given up so much already, I would hate to see you get hurt."

Betty shook her head and found her speech. "No," she said quietly, "I am not worried or afraid, I was only surprised beyond words. When you said you had something to share I expected you to give me your wedding date. You see, I have prayed for weeks that God would help you make a decision and give you your heart's desire."

I stared at her. "How could you have prayed for such a thing? What would have happened to your job if I had moved away?"

Betty shrugged, "I don't know. All I know is that I had obeyed God when I came to work with you. If this ministry were to end, God would have to show me where to go next. I worried more about you. You struggled so hard, and I believe you deserve the best. You deserve to walk into a room on the arm of a handsome, wealthy man who will lay the world at your feet."

"No, Betty," I interrupted her, "I *did* get the best, that is already obvious to me. I have Jesus — and a friend like you. What more do I need?"

That evening I received one more gift. Before I went to sleep the Lord impressed upon me to read Isaiah 54. I had read it before. One text had become especially dear to me ever since our young ministry nearly folded because of the evil one's attacks. So I went right to the text and read it again: "No weapon that is formed against you shall prosper; and every tongue that accuses you in judgment you will condemn" (Isaiah 54:17).

"Now read the whole chapter," the Lord urged me. "All of it is My promise to you!"

I read with growing amazement: "For your husband is your Maker...and your Redeemer is the Holy One of Israel."

My tears rolled again. "Jesus," I said, "I thought this

chapter was written for the nation of Israel alone.
Never would I have dared to apply it to an individual.
Does this now mean that you will be my Husband, dear
Jesus? Who am I to be Your wife? This sounds almost
like an offense to Your majesty and greatness to think
in such terms. It scares me! Do You mean it?

"Don't be afraid," Jesus answered, "I mean every
word you read in the Bible and more."

"Lord, are You willing to be Husband to any single
woman who asks You? Are You Betty's Husband too?"

I almost could see Him smile when He answered. "I
want to be Husband to any woman, single or married. I
want to be best Friend to every man who asks. Yes, I am
Husband to both of you and you can trust Me. I shall
take good care of you just as a loving Husband would."

February/
Monday Before Dawn

Betty and I are in Cairo doing research for a new book on Egypt and the Middle East. Jet lag does strange things to me. I wake up at all hours of the night, and sometimes I just lie still and talk with the Lord. Other times I get up and write or stand out on the hotel balcony to watch the shimmering stars stretching down to the Nile River right below me.

Just two years ago Betty and I had become acquainted on a trip to the Middle East, or to be more specific, to Europe and Israel. People had urged me for a long time to lead a tour to Europe and to include Israel but I hesitated. I had never been farther East than Czechoslovakia, my homeland, and I was not sure what to do about Israel. Would they even permit me to enter? My life story does not encourage such adventure and is too well known in many places through my books.

Born into a German minority group in Czechoslovakia, left as an orphan while still a baby, a shy elderly peasant woman had taken me in because she wanted to raise the waif for Jesus. It didn't seem to work out as she planned because Adolph Hitler made our land part of the German Third Reich and I was chosen to go to a Nazi school in Prague. I left the mountains, the little white cottage, the hayloft I slept in, and my Christian childhood training behind at the age of fourteen and became a brainwashed Nazi youth leader within a few years. It took the shattering end of World War II, my capture and confinement in a Communist labor camp, and a successful escape to Western Germany to bring me back to God and finally to America — my new homeland.

Having lived and raised my family for the last twenty years in the USA, I had apprehensions about taking Americans to Europe. I knew it had changed so much. But Israel was even more disturbing, I knew nothing about the country. Someone suggested a dinner meeting with Betty Pershing, a Bible scholar and specialist on the Holy Land and the Middle East. We met and I was so impressed by her knowledge and wit that I asked her to become our tour leader through Israel while I would be responsible to show the tour group parts of free Europe.

The trip started out with an undercurrent of hostility and tension among some tour members which I had not anticipated. I went to the Lord and said, "Lord, I believe I am leading this tour for You. Some of the people seem to be up-tight, defensive, and critical. What am I doing wrong? Show me what to do differently."

The Lord seemed to say, "Don't worry about it. It is not you who causes the trouble. I will make something beautiful out of it if you just wait and trust Me."

I did not know Betty well at all and would never have shared my concerns with her if I hadn't let a phrase slip one morning while we discussed tour matters. I had learned *not* to use the phrase around strangers, only to my friends: "The Lord told me that..." After I finished the sentence, Betty nodded without surprise in her face and said, "Yes, He told me the same thing."

I swallowed hard. "You mean, Betty, the Lord talks to you, too?"

"Yes," she said. "He has for a long time and when I read your books it made me feel good to know that He spoke to someone else in a similar manner. I often wondered if I was the only oddball among my Christian friends."

From that moment on we began to share and compare many insights. We talked about the tensions in the tour group, we had so painfully observed. The Lord had given her a similar message. Before the trip was over,

Jesus had shown both of us that a spirit of jealousy and the threatened ego of just *one* person had caused most problems. We simply left it with the Lord and trusted Him to handle it, and He did. He not only overruled and drew most of the tour people closer to Himself and to each other, but by the end of the trip Betty and I were friends who respected each other greatly.

What delightful daily Bible teachings she shared. Her great love for Israel found a deep echo in my soul. I came home richly blessed and eager to return to the Middle East to learn more.

Well, here I am two years later, for the first time in Egypt, and next we shall visit Jordan and Israel again. But this trip is free of tension and backbiting, flooded with joy, peace, and harmony! When I walked out to the balcony a few minutes ago I found Betty already at the railing, enjoying the breathtaking beauty.

A full moon glistened over the waters of the Nile and the night hung around me like black velvet. What a romantic scene! I stood enchanted while Betty walked back into the room and returned with her camera. She never said a word. I stood deep in thought talking to the Lord. "Jesus, I said, "this is a honeymoon scene and I am standing here by myself. But I am not sad. It feels right that You are here with me, so very close, so very real, giving me joy and hope and a deep contentment. Thank you, Jesus, and I love You!"

Betty looked up and said quietly, "He will make it up to you." She so often seems to know what I am thinking.

"He has already," I said and went back to the room and to my writing.

"Why would You do all You are doing, Lord?" I asked. "I was prepared to sacrifice and give up everything. I did not do it to trick rewards out of You. You know my heart...!"

"You can never outgive God," Jesus said gently. "Whatever you have given to Me, I will give you back a hundred fold. God is no debtor to anyone. You gave all you had to give. It will be measured to you with the same measure. See what happens when heaven gives you all it has to give in return. I have great plans for you."

I do not know what more heaven could give me. I have so much I can hardly contain it. He gave *all* of it to me at once!

End of March/
Friday Night

We returned from overseas several weeks ago. I am glad to be home but I shall never forget the trip. We had a great time and I learned a lot. The Lord came so close and Betty is a true gift of God to me.

I saw a different side of her on this last trip. I knew her only as an easygoing person, but in Egypt I discovered a quiet strength and firmness that surprised me and some people who don't know her very well. She carries an iron hand in a velvet glove when dealing with the public. She believes strongly that God called her to serve Him and to look after me. She told me herself that Jesus had made her double calling crystal clear to her. And she takes both tasks most seriously, I found out.

Sometimes people can wear out a public figure with too much kindness, but in Egypt they can do so without trying to be kind. Our Egyptian guides were typical Middle Eastern men who on their very best behavior treated us like mindless objects. After all we were only women. They felt we could be pushed around, and most of the time we didn't protest too much, we understood. But on a few occasions I watched Betty not only bristle but put her foot down. Whenever she thought that someone tried to "use" me or show me off from place to place without consideration of my need to eat or rest, she could even get furious.

I still chuckle every time I remember one long morning when "Mister Important" had driven us to every place except to the sights we wanted to see. Both of us had tried hard to remain polite, attentive, and gracious as we met all his "friends." We had gone two hours past

lunch time. He had even hurried us too much that
morning to catch a decent breakfast before leaving on
the tour. Betty reached over and touched my hands. I
get clammy, ice-cold hands when my blood sugar gets
too low and I fight light dizzy spells if I don't eat on
time.

She nodded grimly and said to our Egyptian host,
"Please, return immediately to our hotel for food." She
spoke quietly but firmly. I wondered if anyone had even
heard, the guide and chauffeur conversed loudly without paying any attention to us. We also did not drive the
normal route to our hotel. Suddenly the car stopped, the
Egyptian jumped out and opened our car door.

"It will take only a few minutes to meet the US
ambassador. I have made an appointment for you."

We looked at each other. His "appointment" line
was getting familiar. We suspected it was another one
of his tall tales. We found out later we were right. He
was simply trying to use me so that he could meet the
ambassador himself. I waited for a signal from Betty.
Should I try to make one more stop?

She said quietly but icily, "No! We shall *not* stop here,
but proceed immediately to the hotel. We are not going
anyplace but to the next dining room to eat."

I will never forget the startled look on our guide's
face. He did not know that any woman could have the
nerve to oppose a man's command. I bit my lip so as not
to smile and, of course, I didn't move. The gentleman
grumbled something, closed his door — and we drove
straight to the hotel.

What a wonderful thing to have the Lord and a caring
friend like her on my side. By now I carry a new
assurance within me. I shall never be alone again,
neither in good nor in bad times. I also know that the
sun doesn't always shine.

I had absolutely no inkling about the first major
crisis we three, the Lord, Betty, and I, would face
together. It came only days after we had returned from
overseas.

I felt great, and even the return jet lag didn't get me down. My new closeness with the Lord and all the evidence of His care and love had obviously put a glow on my face, that even I was not aware of. At a meeting with a top executive of one of my American publishers right after I got home we discussed a manuscript I had just signed over to him. He looked into my face and said, "If I hadn't read the last chapter of your new book, I would have to believe you are in love."

I beamed and meant every word when I answered, "I am in love! I have never been deeper in love in all my life. Jesus is my Husband and He is sufficient for everything."

Little did I know what lay ahead that would put my words to the test.

Arrangements had been completed for Betty and me to leave for Palm Springs shortly. I often write there, hidden away in a small desert hotel, removed from interruptions and the constant ringing of the telephone. The newly gathered material on the Middle East had to be processed immediately. We had only three short weeks left before preparing for various and separate speaking appointments. We needed to sort out our research material. The Lord made it clear and very urgent that we get the manuscript done as fast as possible.

I felt sick the morning of our planned departure. It was not my usual morning grogginess or an uneasy stomach which I often experience since I had my ulcer surgery years ago. I felt strangely dizzy, disoriented, I couldn't even focus my eyes. Betty had to teach another Bible class before we left at noon. She poked her head into my bedroom and I told her I didn't feel too good and would take it a bit easy.

"Shall I stay with you?" she asked with obvious concern.

"No," I tried to smile. "I know Jesus wants you to teach your class, I asked Him already."

She must have gotten the same message and I

watched her leave, but I could sense her reluctance.

I forced myself to get up and go downstairs to see if Peter was ready for school and to tell him goodbye. Dragging to the couch in the living room, I laid down.

Peter looked upset. "Mom," he said, "you look terrible. Do you want me to stay with you?"

"No," I said between dry heaves, "please leave immediately for school or you will be late. I will be OK. Jesus is with me!" He kissed me and left, literally dragging his big feet.

The house was empty and deathly still and I felt myself going down into half consciousness and deeper spasms of nausea. "Lord," I pleaded silently, "if I go into one of my vomiting spells, I cannot stop, You know that. I have always ended up in the hospital in the past with it. What do You want me to do?"

"You can either go to the hospital or trust Me. I will see you through." The Lord spoke into my befuddled thinking.

"I'd rather fall into Your hands any day, Jesus," I whispered, "but You know what my stomach can do to me, and I am alone in the house."

"I am with you," the Lord assured me, "and I promise you, I will see you through!"

For hours my body heaved and I could feel myself slip toward unconsciousness. But every time I would call out to Jesus He would be right there to calm my fears and bring me back. By the time Betty walked into the house the Lord said, "The worst is over!" My spasms came at longer intervals and less violently.

I said, "What next, Jesus?"

He said, "Leave for Palm Springs as planned or go to the hospital."

"We'll go to Palm Springs," I told Betty. She didn't argue but tried to protest when I sat up to get ready. "The Lord told me to pack my own overnight case," I said feebly, "so I better obey."

I crawled up the stairs and laid flat on the bathroom floor, I was so dizzy. I got one toilet article at a time, rested and reached for the next. Betty stood beside me in obvious agony but never interfered with my activities.

I cannot remember that I had ever in all my life had to try harder to make my body move. I felt a slow paralysis grip me from head to toe and I had an overpowering desire to just let go and fall into a soft darkness. But I gritted my teeth and kept on doing what I thought the Lord wanted me to do.

Betty packed books, the typewriter and some clothing, and helped me into the front seat of her car. The rest of the story I got from her later.

After she had locked the house and gotten into the driver's seat, I laid down and put my head in her lap. My head hurt so badly I thought it would burst. She put her warm hand over my forehead and steered the car with the other hand. She never stopped talking to the Lord while she drove the 120 miles to Palm Springs.

First, she asked Jesus to drive and keep the speed limit. Next, she asked Him if it was all right if I fell asleep. The Lord assured her it would make me feel better. I slept all the way and Betty didn't do anything to waken me. She drove in silence and conversed in her heart with our divine Husband. "What happened to her?" she asked over and over. The Lord's answer puzzled her. He said, "Don't let fear come in. If fear is allowed to enter, Satan will destroy her."

"Destroy her, Lord?" Betty asked. "Is she that sick?"

"Yes, she is very sick," Jesus said, "but you can trust Me. I will see her through and the worst is over. Her recovery will take time, but she will be fine."

By the time we arrived in Palm Springs the nausea attacks had stopped. I was just so horribly dizzy. I didn't want the motel proprietor to think I was drunk so I grabbed Betty's arm. I walked rather slowly but straight, and with my head held very high, into our suite.

By evening I managed to swallow some oatmeal, my faithful standby in times of stomach turmoil. Betty never left my side. I was still too groggy to wonder why she posted herself close to the bathroom door when I brushed my teeth.

I slept fitfully, dreamed horrible nightmares, and every time I woke up, Betty was bending over me, searching my face. She never told me until several days later what the Lord had told her.

For days the dizziness persisted so badly that I couldn't walk unaided. But I managed to get from my bed to a chair on the porch, asked for my writing pad and said, "Lord, I'll hold the pencil and You write. We came here to finish a manuscript and the old devil will not stop us!"

The Lord did write and the little book did get finished within the three weeks.*

By now we are back home and I am trying to fit the pieces together. I am still weak and dizzy but I can move around as long as I do things the slow and easy way.

I talked to a longtime nurse on the phone the other day about my strange sickness and she asked, "Did you eat in any restaurant before it happened?"

"Yes," I said, "We stopped in a Mexican restaurant for lunch while running last minute errands."

My friend suggested that the symptoms pointed to severe food poisoning, most likely botulism. The stuff can be and has often proven fatal to unsuspecting victims.

Thanks to a wonderful Lord and a faithful friend like Betty I lived to tell the story. How blessed I am!

* See *Will the Eastwind Blow,* published by Hansi Ministries.

April/*Monday Evening*

I am preparing to leave for the Midwest for several weeks of speaking engagements. Betty has several appointments here on the West Coast. So we decided that Cheri, our office manager, would travel with me for the first three weeks until Betty could fly east to meet me. We have a joint speaking appointment at a Sunday School convention. Everybody thinks I am still too weak to travel alone and I do not argue. I feel dizzy most of the time and tire more easily than usual.

Several issues had to be settled in my home and my own heart before I could leave. First, I had to have a long talk with my divine Husband. I asked Him if I had been deathly sick with food poisoning. The Lord agreed.

"Lord," I said, "we have just come back from Egypt and Jordan and I did not have the slightest problem in spite of polluted water and other bad bugs. Why did it hit me here in America instead?"

"You did your very best in Egypt to be careful and avoid contamination," the Lord explained, "and I watched over you to keep you both well."

"And what makes the difference between overseas and getting caught here in America?" I asked bewildered.

"You didn't *ask* Me what to eat in that restaurant, did you?" the Lord said as lovingly as always.

His words struck me. "You mean I should *ask* before I order food in any restaurant? Do I dare bother You with such small daily matters? Is it even right for me to do so?" My thoughts tumbled, I was so surprised and overwhelmed by His new teachings.

"You don't have to, but you can ask Me if you wish." the Lord continued ever so patiently. "Nothing is too small or too big for Me. I am glad to help you with

anything, and you save yourself a lot of problems if you
ask Me. I would be glad to warn you of any harm. All
you need to do is *ask*! So often My children have not
because they ask not."

I told Betty and she said, "You can be sure from now
on we not only say Grace before meals, but also *ask*
what to eat. I am so sorry I did not think of it before. It
appears so simple and clear in the light of Scripture.
Why must we so often learn the hard way."

Next, I had to have a talk with my sons. I had asked
the Lord about something that really puzzled me.
"Jesus," I said, "I have been wondering for weeks now,
ever since it happened. Why did you give me such clear
orders to leave for Palm Springs the day I got so terribly
sick? Couldn't I have stayed in my familiar surroundings and left after I recovered a bit?"

"No," the Lord answered, "I had to get you out of your
house. Too much satanic power..."

"Did I hear you right, Jesus?" I shivered. "Are You
telling me that Satan has evil spirits in *my* house? How
can that be? How did they get in? You are the Head of
our home, dear Lord. Every morning Betty and I pray
together and read our Bible..."

"Demonic spirits have entered your home for a long
time through your children's records," the Lord spoke
very clearly. "Some types of music open the door in your
home and many other Christian homes to satanic
attacks!"

I simply told my children about my conversation
with the Lord. They and I have had an agreement
through many stormy years that everybody must keep
his or her stereo music soft and confined to his own
room when I am at home. But Betty and I are fully
aware that the house rocks and the speakers blare full
blast when we're not around. All my children went
through the "rock-age." It began with the "Beatles."
Now I hear about "Kiss," "Styx," "Rolling Stones" and
"Punk Rock." My son and I don't see eye to eye on the
subject, but we do not argue.

"I had no intention to do anyone any harm with my music," he said seriously.

"I am not telling you what to do, son," I said and tried to be as gentle as possible. "I am also not suggesting that every piece of music that carries a beat is satanic. All I am asking you, honey, would you please think it through."

He nodded and went into his room. Later I watched him walk out with an armful of records. I knew he didn't get rid of all his albums, but I have to trust him. I believe he loves me enough that the Lord and he must have come to terms what to take out of the house and what to keep.

The Lord Jesus is becoming more and more the Head of this home, as I learn "to let go and let God" take charge as a husband should. Things go better with my children since I started to talk to God about them instead of talking to them about God. I have stopped preaching and nagging.

I even began to ask the Lord of the universe to help me with the mundane things of a household. I wondered if I acted irreverently when I turned to Him a while ago and said, "Lord, I don't know what to do about the rain leak in the dining room whenever the back porch floods. The water doesn't seem to come in through the sliding doors, it seeps up from below and soaks the carpet. Wouldn't a husband take care of such things?"

"Go to the toolbox," the Lord said. "Take the white tube." I picked it up and wondered what it contained. I must have brought it along years ago when I dissolved our home after the breakup. It was some kind of a tub sealer, hardened at the top. The Lord suggested to cut the other side open and salvage enough soft paste to fill in a crack between the cement and the door sill that I had never noticed before. After I had done the sealing I looked at the dark sky and said aloud, "If it rains before the stuff dries, it will wash out, Lord. And it looks like we'll have a downpour any minute."

"I'll take care of it," the Lord assured me and I went

inside to attend to my many duties. I did not remember my sealed crack until I returned from the office in the evening and told Betty. We checked and it was hard and dry. Rain poured the whole night and we had rainy weeks since then but we never had another bit of moisture appear! Thank You, Jesus.

Some people would argue with me that the whole thing was common sense and a coincidence, but I know better. I don't have that kind of common sense. I am rather helpless when it comes to fixing things or running a household by myself. I did not even know how to write a check, balance a budget, and had just learned to drive a car before our home broke up. The Lord is teaching me patiently and sensibly — not by my good sense, but His, and I know it.

This weekend we had another serious problem. We could smell the smoldering of electrical wires around Peter's bathroom. We searched, checked wires, and unplugged extension cords, but the pungent odor persisted. I wondered what would happen in case of fire; Peter would soon be alone in the house. Betty and I went out and bought a smoke alarm and installed it right over Peter's bedroom door. The lad sleeps like a bear and I wondered if he would wake up in time to escape — nothing wakes him. I bought him the loudest alarm clock I could find and he sleeps right through it, though the blaring ring wakens us upstairs.

I talked to the Lord several times about the electrical problem and every time I got the same answer: "I will take care of it."

I finally said, "With all respect, dear Lord, what do You mean? I cannot find an electrician willing to come to the house over the weekend and on such short notice. Neither can we tear the house apart to find the faulty wire, what am I to do?"

"I will take care of it," the Lord repeated and I wondered and prayed some more. "Jesus," I finally said, "I don't understand but I trust You, even with a utility problem."

Sunday night the light did not switch on in the bathroom and the smell was gone. I felt great relief and told my son he would have to live without a ceiling light until Betty and I returned from tour. The wire had obviously burned through and we would bring in a repair man as soon as I was home again. Peter was not excited at the prospect of weeks without decent light in his bathroom but he was willing to adjust.

This morning I walked into Peter's bathroom before he was awake and, by habit, I flipped the light switch. The light came on. I smelled, checked, turned the light off and on several times and all appeared normal. I turned to the Lord and said, absolutely astonished, "Jesus, the light is working and all seems well. I didn't expect this."

He said, "I told you I would take care of it. Now stop worrying."

I cried and laughed at the same time and I thanked Him over and over. "Forgive me, Lord," I said aloud. "I know I worry too much. It is clear that You are willing to take care of everything, even if it is not a spiritual matter. To think that You would even fix a light switch!"

"Wouldn't a good husband do that," the Lord of the universe said ever so tenderly, and I felt His arm around me so very close!

End of May/
Saturday Night

The days fly by so fast I cannot keep up with all the events. The speaking tour went just fine and I discovered something great: Betty and I do well as team speakers. The audience at the Sunday School convention apparently loved the way we taught together. Betty presents a subject from the Biblical view, I approach it as a psychologist in a practical way. It takes both sides to make a topic sparkle and the enthusiastic response took us by surprise. The mail is still coming in and we got several invitations to speak together. I told my office staff to encourage such double appointments. People need to hear Betty's Bible teaching, she is the best!

So far, we still go, for the most part, in separate directions for our various speaking engagements. May is banquet month and Betty has been in great demand as a banquet speaker for many years. Ever since we returned from the Midwest we have been driving busily all over Southern California. Betty drove her old Pontiac. I used the Scout owned by the ministry because I had given my own little MG sports car to Tim. He in turn gave the girls his Volkswagen. Peter, at the end, got the girls' little ailing jalopy because he had the shortest distance to drive. Just to keep all my children rolling to school and work and pay for the various insurances has kept me humble and leaning on my Lord for financial wisdom.

Well, Peter had another breakdown and Betty let him drive her car to work after school on a day when she didn't need to go out. The next day the Pontiac sounded terrible. Peter pleaded innocence. We rolled the vehicle to our trusted mechanic. He checked it and said, "Get rid of it — and now!"

We had several problems. First, Betty needed a car fast, within two days, according to her appointment calendar. Second, we did not have enough cash to buy another car off the lot and she would have to have her credit approved. I have absolutely no credit established because I am a recently divorced woman and nobody trusts me even with the smallest credit card.

So, we prayed together. Betty said, "Lord neither of us is mechanically minded or experienced in car buying. This is a husband's responsibility. We are asking You to pick the car, lead us to the place, and make the financial arrangements."

I added: "Lord, if it is not too much to ask, we need a car the day after tomorrow."

The Lord said, "Make a list of what you want on your next car." So Betty and I wrote on a piece of paper our requests: cruise control, a closed trunk to discourage thievery (our office manager's compact car had just been broken into), a cassette deck for our music tapes, power steering and brakes, good gas mileage but a strong enough motor to pass safely, of USA make, to help the economy. Almost as an afterthought I added: bucket seats, and color of car — gray or blue.

Betty and I went to several car lots and read our list to the various salesmen. We got no encouragement. One fellow was downright rude. "Ladies," he said, "you are just plain dreaming. We have very few models left and the new cars will not be in until September. You better buy what you can get. You don't have a chance in a million to get what you're asking for."

By late afternoon we felt tired and discouraged. We had looked and prayed and nothing seemed to come our way. There was one lot we had not visited because someone had told me never to drive a car of that make. In desperation we finally walked into the showroom and were met by a very courteous salesman. We liked him! I read our list but left off the last two items. He went through his file and said thoughtfully: "I believe I have the exact car you want. Come and see."

I bit my lip to avoid asking about the color or the seats. We walked out and found our new car waiting for us — of course, with bucket seats and in a beautiful blue-gray, which is Betty's favorite color.

Yes, the credit was arranged within one day too, and Betty drove our new car to her next speaking appointment. We have been cruising in it a lot lately and it drives like a dream! I would never tell people to follow our way of buying a car or anything else for that matter, but we have so little time and no experience in so many areas, we have nobody to lean on but the Lord. We either trust Him or go on forever wondering if we shouldn't have looked more, asked for advice, picked something else...?

For peace of mind it is better to trust Him completely, especially after a thing is done. I realize that our humanness always leaves a possibility open that we do not hear the Lord right or interpret his words incorrectly, but He makes provision even for that. Isaiah 61:3 tells us that He can bring good out of our mistakes, beauty out of ashes, garlands of joy out of mourning. I love that Old Testament Bible text, and Romans 8:28 becomes more and more meaningful, too. Jesus can make something good out of everything, not for everybody, but for those who love Him and are called according to His purpose.

It is His greatest purpose to see all His human children saved, so He would love to work "all things" out for everybody, but so many troubled souls will not let Him.

I am thinking of a family who lived a few houses down from us. I had gotten acquainted with them when I moved here and found out they were Christians. The main reason I got involved was their need for help. It was another marriage on the rocks. For some reason people seem to come to me for family counseling and it surprises me. Why would someone ask *me* for help in family matters after my own marriage failed.

I watched my neighbors' home go completely to pieces and it was a messy divorce. I pleaded with both sides to handle it with more human dignity, but nobody listened. The children paid the biggest price. I know because they would come and talk to me. I tried to explain to them that their parents did not mean to hurt them but were so deeply involved in their own conflict that they couldn't see their children's confusion.

Every divorce is different, but so very alike in many ways. Whenever and wherever a home breaks up, the great enemy of souls brings in a spirit of rejection and betrayal; former love and trust is belittled, denied, or misused. One of the patterns I have observed is that in every split there seems to be a "winner" and a "loser," an "initiator" and a "victim." The loser or victim seems to end up with more self-pity, bitterness and resentment. In my neighbors' case the husband saw himself victimized. The wife packed up and moved to the other end of town. The children bounced between the two parents.

For the children's sake I tried to stand by, but sometimes it would get me down. The man's endless complaining would send everybody running, which only made him more bitter and resentful against the whole wide world.

So often when I listen to divorced people who, just like him, have not one good word to say about their former partner, I wonder if they wiped out part of their past in their memories. Most couples begin with a deep commitment. They have children because they unite in love. They create a unique family togetherness filled with good and not so good memories. Suddenly *all* comes to nothing except those episodes that prove the villain's evilness.

For a while I tried my best to tell the angry man that he could not put down his former wife in front of his children. He not only destroyed their respect for their mother but also their own self-esteem. Every child becomes half victim and half villain in such a conflict, and so often kids have no other choice but to withdraw from both sides.

I also try hard to find some time to visit with the woman, mostly over the phone. She knows that I am still attempting to fit the pieces of my own shattered life together and is aware that I don't have all the answers by far, but we seem to have a "comradery in sorrow." Contrary to popular opinion I see her as the better Christian of the two. My neighbor has the full support of his church. After all, she left him! He attends church more regularly than ever while she stays home. Hers is a very lonely home. By financial necessity the children live mostly with him. They also wish to stay in the school in our neighborhood. They grew up here and longtime peers have become more important than ever.

I encouraged Lydia not to defend or revenge herself in front of her children. From my own experience I know that the only key to healing is forgiveness. She agrees with me that no home breaks up just because *one* party is *all* at fault. We are all so human! She knows of her mistakes — and I do of mine! God is willing to mend anything but He cannot begin unless *we* are willing to forgive first.

My angry neighbor does not agree, though he is a professing Christian. His Bible seems to have different texts than mine. According to some remarks his children made to me, he was not going to church to worship anyway. He met a woman there who seems to be everything he ever dreamed of. She is divorced, too, has children, and appears to be blessed with the sweetest, most agreeable personality anyone could wish for. He married her only months after his divorce was final. They had a big church wedding. I did not attend, I simply couldn't. I am not against remarriage. I believe it must always be a personal matter between God and the couple or individual, and nobody has a right to decide for another what to do or not to do. But why is it a common Christian belief that people are *always* put

together by God just because they were united in a
church wedding?

According to my neighbor's children, she, the new
stepmother, chased him until he caught her. I was
concerned because he got married so soon, even after he
had assured me repeatedly that he did not do it on the
rebound, never! He was above such juvenile behavior!
She treated me from the start with great friendliness,
and like a long lost friend. It put me on guard. I like my
friendships to evolve and grow more slowly. To say the
least, I was intrigued to watch this remarriage. But the
longer I observed some things, the more I began to
worry and wonder. My neighbor and his new wife
appear so different, I cannot help but question if they
have anything in common. I must have expressed
myself in that line because one of their teenage girls
gave me an answer. She said it in a half-joking way:
"They have nothing in common but one thing: they
hate their former mates." The words struck me so hard,
I couldn't even smile.

"Oh, Lord," I thought, "two victims are nursing their
unforgiveness as a foundation to a new marriage. How
long can it last?"

Well, so far as I know it is still lasting. They moved
just a little while ago and his children blame her. She
wanted a bigger house and I wondered why. She had
griped to me about all the cleaning she had to do in his
house. Too bad, the kids lost their peer group after all. I
have an invitation to visit them if I am ever in their
neighborhood, but I am not eager to do so. The whole
situation gets to me. Her sweet and easygoing personality didn't last too long either. She nags and yells a lot
— when she thinks no stranger is listening.

I will never forget one morning shortly after my
neighbor had come back with her from the honeymoon.
I was out jogging with my poodle and passed their
home. I heard a screaming voice and wondered if my
friends had an emergency. I walked up to the door and
listened. The new stepmother was giving her combined

family a piece of her mind and every scolding word
pierced the still morning air through the open window.
I was not sure if I could get away undetected, so I rang
the bell. The door opened and a smiling composed
woman greeted me, speaking ever so softly and apparently "in love" with everybody. I couldn't believe the
peaceful "perfect" family I saw before me: husband and
wife holding hands, the children all smiles. I murmured
some idiotic reason for stopping, excused myself and
hurried home. My mind reeled.

"Lord," I said, "someone is playing a charade in that
house. I surely would like to know why all this sweet
pretending is so important."

If I understood the Lord correctly, He said, "Their
unforgiving spirit compels both to play 'happy home'
before outsiders. They must prove to everybody, and to
their former partners, that they have finally arrived in
total bliss."

I ached for them, I still do. What will happen when
their energy is spent and they cannot pretend any
longer? Every marriage hits some rough spots no
matter how compatible and "put together by God" the
couple is. Human imperfection sometimes makes any
relationship a trial, and it takes hard work to adjust
and integrate.

I remember when I asked one of my divorced and
remarried preacher friends if he found his second
marriage less trying and more fulfilling. Were they
more compatible?

"Any marriage has its own set of problems," he said
with a wistful smile. "So people exchange one set of
problems for another. The reason why it appears
smoother is because both partners are trying harder to
make it work the second time around. My wife and I
agree that if we had tried as hard the first time as we do
in this marriage, we both might have saved our first
marriages."

I read a saying that suggested when two people
remarry, four people climb into bed. I think its more

than that, especially when children are involved. The absent partners are always looking over someone's shoulder. What a miserable life when unforgiveness and hate keep shadows in every corner and skeletons in every closet — and so often in the name of a loving Christ.

Lately I find myself praying for my former husband and his fiancee. I saw them both at Tim's graduation just a while ago and I know we will meet again in a few days at Peter's high school graduation. My children mentioned that Dad will get married within the next few weeks.

There is no need to describe the mixture of feelings when a woman sees the father of her children with another woman on his arm. All I know is that I cannot let bitterness or resentment poison my life. And I pray that both of them begin their new home in a spirit of forgiveness and love. The Lord knows my heart. I wish them happiness and fulfillment of their hearts' desires, and I mean it!

June/*Sunday Afternoon*

We just returned from a staff outing in Santa Barbara. At first, I wondered why Betty and the rest of the staff insisted on this date, then Peter and Tim mentioned that they would be gone for the weekend to attend Dad's wedding. So I agreed to a "fun day" and we all tried our best to make each other laugh and forget.

On the way home we sat in our shiny new car, just Betty and I, and I let the tears roll. I am thankful to God for tears and for a friend like Betty. She never said a word, but let me cry out my unspoken hurts, and by the time we arrived at our home I felt better.

Betty and I are preparing for another overseas trip and I am so glad Tim is staying in our home at least for the summer. He graduated and is looking for an apartment. Peter will go to a Christian college this fall and live in the dormitory. It is good that the two boys can be together for a few months, it helps both of them.

I thank the Lord that Tim is staying near us. He almost ended up in faraway Texas. I'll never forget the evening he called me, a few weeks before his graduation. His grade point average put him at the top of his class as a chemical engineer and the big oil companies had come to interview and hire the cream of the graduation class. Tim received a lucrative offer from an oil giant in Texas and he wondered if he should accept it. It was one of the very few times I lost my composure. I cried on the phone and said, "Son, if you leave please take your younger brother along. He looks up to you, he needs you, and I need a man's advice on how to handle Peter." I cried so hard I had to say goodbye and hang up.

Tim called back a few days later and said, "Mom, I want you to know that I turned down my Texas offer. I have accepted a job here on the West Coast and I'll stick around for a few years. Stop worrying so much, OK?" Needless to say, I cried again. My oldest son and I have come a long way together.

My mind goes back to the time when he was born in Germany. He was only three years old when we immigrated to America. He and his six-year-old sister were model children. Today I realize they did not have much of a choice. I was an overly strict mother and thought I had all the answers to child-rearing. Any problem could be solved with strict discipline. For the first six years here in America my philosophy seemed to work. By then three more children had come to join our family, and from their births on I could notice a difference between their behavior and that of my two oldest children. It's almost as though there is something in the air in America that encourages children to act up. I wondered about it but was not overly concerned. I had full confidence that I was still in perfect control.

When Tina became a teenager, I had no forewarning of what lay ahead of me. She suddenly began to reason with me in earnest. She dared to suggest that nylons and high heels might not be of the devil.

I simply cut her off. "White socks and oxfords are healthier for you."

"Mom," she would try again another day, "other girls use some mascara and their mothers permit it."

I figured that my stern answers had convinced my child and settled the argument. They hadn't! Instead, they just encouraged my teenage girl to live with a double standard. She learned to wash the mascara off before coming home from school and to do other things behind my back. I never suspected anything.

When Tim hit teenage, more than three years later, I still hadn't caught on that I was not in perfect control. Tim's rebellion took me by complete surprise. I did not expect it because he had been a "model" child. He exploded in my smug face and I watched in disbelief as my gentle, obedient, intelligent boy became a rebel almost overnight. He suddenly seemed to make it his highest challenge in life to outtalk me, outsmart me, and to convince himself and the three younger children that I was a crazy, old-fashioned woman who belonged in a "nut house."

"Mother," he would growl in his changing voice, "this is America, OK? Things are different here than they were in *your* land." He sounded as if I had come from the moon. My three smaller youngsters listened carefully and learned.

The battles we fought while Tim grew into adulthood are too numerous and painful to mention. His dad was seldom around. His occupation brought him home on weekends only. By necessity I had to handle most of the discipline. It didn't seem fair to save up the weekly problems for his arrival.

I had also gone back to college during these years and fought many other difficulties, but none of them more traumatic than Tim's change of attitude. I could not begin to count the sleepless nights I spent praying, pleading and agonizing before God.

"Please, Lord," I would beg, "show me where I failed. I tried so hard to do my best with the children. I had family worship every day. The only music I allowed in the house was religious records. I took all of them, from birth on, faithfully to church and taught them many songs and Bible verses. I did not permit them to copy the world. I plead with You, oh, God, to teach me at any cost. I have three more children growing up and I can't bear the thought that every one of them will follow the same rebellious pattern."

I found out that God will teach us if we are willing to learn. Sometimes it is a painful process to see our unintentional mistakes. And when we try to correct them it takes time, and we must learn patience with ourselves first.

God showed me that my greatest error was my misconception about my children's freedom of choice. I had struggled with the concept of freedom ever since I had come to America.

Freedom in any shape or form was new to me. In the first years of our stay in this country I had often been frightened by it. I came from a background which had taught me that obedience without questioning was the highest virtue of human life. From babyhood on I was told when and what to think and to do. Nobody ever permitted or encouraged me to think for myself or to make my own decisions until I came to America as a grown-up woman.

I raised my children the way I was taught. Children should be seen not heard. I thought I had made the ultimate adjustment to the new "free" life style in America when I allowed my children to express their opinions. Where I grew up, a child wasn't even allowed to speak to an adult unless he was addressed first. (Very seldom did someone bother to speak to a little orphan girl!) To give my children a true choice or vote in the matters of their young lives never entered my head. I had planned their education, professions, and spiritual journey from the moment I knelt beside each one of my new born children and dedicated them to the Lord. For Him I would raise them!

Looking back I can see now how for years the Lord had tried to give me glimpses of the meaning and source of all freedom. He Himself gave it at the beginning of time. He lovingly gave it to all His children, angels and humans alike. Love cannot be served by force or fear. Love always gives and responds to free choice. Jesus died to give the human race its freedom back. After the first sin, Satan had taken everyone on earth captive and freedom was lost. Next to salvation, freedom of choice is God's greatest gift to mankind. Nobody can touch it without displeasing God. I violated one of God's greatest spiritual laws when I tried to live my children's lives for them.

"You have tried to brainwash your children," Jesus said to me one night. "Someone brainwashed you as a teenager and now you try to do the same."

"But, Lord," I argued back, "I try to teach them the right way. I was taught a lie. Isn't there a difference?"

"It is never right to force anyone, not even to make them go My way," God said to me.

I never felt more bewildered. "Lord," I asked, "don't I have to keep firm rules in the house? I can't permit my children to do as they please. They are not mature enough to know what is best for them. They could go wild...!"

The Lord showed me that I had to make a difference between setting up sensible rules and forcing my children to follow *my* way of thinking. Rules are essential in any home. Parents must reinforce them consistently to give their children the needed security which comes from order and structure. But nobody has a right to do the thinking for another person. Teenagers are capable of conceptual thinking and begin to develop their own reasoning power. They often have no other chance to learn but by their own mistakes. We parents do the same with our Father — God. He gave His human children good rules to point us all toward a fulfilled abundant life. Has He ever forced anyone to keep His rules? Whenever we think that we know better than God, and break the laws of a Godly life, we have to take the consequences of our behavior. But even then God never lets us down or turns away. He always stands gently and soothingly by. He even changes our self-made crosses into a blessing if we let Him. God will never force anything on us, not even His love.

I learned ever so slowly but surely. For my two oldest children my insights seemed to come too late. The damage was done. Tina turned bitter against a Puritan God whom she perceived as revengeful, spoiling all fun and was out to punish her harshly for any mistake.

Tim went further than that. When I put the choice before him to either abide by the rules of our home or leave, he moved out. He stayed with some friends who proclaimed the "new morality" by their life style of free sex, dope, and alcohol. For a while Tim dropped out of college, an expensive private church university, chosen against his will by his parents. When he finally went back to school he decided to go to a junior college.

I swallowed my professional pride and told him I was proud of him and every good grade he made. After that he picked up his own special training at a technical state school to become a scientist. It's a far cry from the dream I had for him. I raised him to be a missionary doctor.

When I understood that I had no right to force my dreams on my children, I found a new respect for them. I not only encouraged them to reach out after their own goals but I made it a special point to ask both Tina and Tim to forgive me for my many great mistakes.

I found out that young people are more tolerant and willing to let bygones be bygones than we older ones often are. Today, Tina and I are good friends and Tim communicates with me again. I have learned to listen more and preach less. My son has given me great insights into the thinking of his generation.

"Look, Mom," he said one day when he was visiting between semesters, "my generation has a different outlook toward the future than you had when you were my age. We look toward adulthood and see the mushroom cloud of a nuclear war in the distance."

Another time we talked about his high school days and he said, "Mom, I tried to please you, but I never could come up to your demands. Your standards were unreachable..."

My tears rolled when I told him again how sorry I was because I had tried to force and manipulate him toward my ideas and religious experiences.

He said kindly, "Look, Mom, don't torture yourself anymore. You did what you thought was best at the time. Have you forgotten what the Bible says?"

I stood mentally on tiptoe, wondering what he would quote. Lately he had declared himself an agnostic and denied any divine inspiration of the Bible. I couldn't believe he even remembered any Bible texts any more.

He smiled and said, "Train up a child in the way he should go and when he is old he will not depart from it." Then he grinned broadly and added, "Give me time, Mother. I'm not old yet."

Well, I am willing to give all my children all the time they need. I try hard to be more balanced with the three younger children. I don't nag or preach constantly. If I feel I need to talk to any of my children about a sensitive issue, I go first to talk to God about them.

Whenever I counsel or share with the many troubled parents I find across the land, I try to point out some encouraging facts I have discovered the hard way. The more intelligent a child is, the more rebellion can be expected. Parental teaching comes to a sudden stop at teenage time, seed-sowing normally is finished by the age of twelve. After that our children know what we are thinking. They have heard us for more than a decade. Young people resent it when we don't give them credit that they can think for themselves. They respond better if we make an effort to praise them for anything they try to do right, even if they do it differently than we would.

Right now I listen to my older son give his younger brother much sensible advice. I can't believe how much Tim has changed in the last few years. But he has the same idea about me. On one of our recent walks on the beach he turned to me and said, "I can't believe how much you have learned in the last few years, Mom."

Well, neither can I!

November/*Saturday after Thanksgiving*

The year is soon coming to an end and I can't believe how swiftly the weeks have turned themselves into a kaleidoscope of memories. So much has happened since June.

Our summer tour to Israel and Austria will always stay vividly in my mind. Betty and I decided to take our two young men along. The trip was their graduation present. Ever since I had visited Israel for the first time I longed to take my children there. It is amazing how Jesus, like a loving indulgent husband, gives me more and more the desires of my heart.

We have until next year to pay off the boys' fare and we thought it worthwhile to go into debt for it. I shall never regret it and I promised the girls the same treat as soon as they graduate. By the time they do so our finances should be stabilized again.

On our return from Israel we spent two nights in Munich, which is in the southern part of Germany. Tim was born there and I wanted him to know his roots. My children's father and his new wife were spending their honeymoon at his sister's place so the boys got to meet relatives they had never met before. All in all it was an exciting time for them, bittersweet for me, and Jesus held me very near to Himself.

Now Peter is off to college and Tim started work in another beach city, but he still lives in our house. He drives a long way in heavy traffic and it concerns me. He is looking for an apartment near his oil company.

Betty and I had some urgent business to attend to between our speaking appointments this fall. A day before we left for another three-week tour she got a check. Betty had resigned from her nearly lifelong employment to work for our young ministry. Though she had lost her retirement benefits she was eligible for a refund of the retirement money she had paid in for more than twenty years. The cover letter with the substantial check advised her to invest the money within sixty days or she would have to pay heavy taxes.

Tim suggested we use it as a down payment for a small home. How does one find a suitable place within two months? Aren't eight weeks long enough? Certainly not, when both of us are scheduled to be on tour for three months with only ten days back on the West Coast within those next sixty days.

* * * * * * * *

While we finished our three weeks of serving together on the East Coast, Betty and I prayed and planned a lot. We knew what we wanted in a home but we were sensible enough to face the facts. Our dreams and the available cash did not match. I assured Betty that we simply would not move back into heavy smog areas. Both of us are allergic to Los Angeles' visible air. But beach properties were beyond our means. Where could we move? The mountains' winter roads had posed problems in the past. I had no encouragement from the Lord to move back "up."

"Jesus," I would say, "it looks impossible. We don't want to live in the city, the beach is out of reach, the mountains not practical. Are we listening right? Are we supposed to buy a home?"

"I have it all picked out and prepared for you," the Lord assured me. "I will lead you to it."

We returned from the airport, dropped our luggage and packed a small overnight case. It was late Friday afternoon and Betty settled herself behind the wheel of our new car. We were on our way to find the home Jesus had already picked and reserved for us. Betty looked at me, "Which way shall we go?"

"To the beach," I said.

When we approached Pacific Coast Highway she

said, "north or south?"

I said, "If I understand the Lord correctly, it's south." She nodded and we drove in silence. I wondered if Jesus had a certain area in mind that was not very fancy because industry had ruined the view and the beach. The properties there were still prohibitive but some little shabby hut might be for sale and affordable.

I mentioned it to Betty. She had thought the same thing. Both of us did not feel very excited about living near smokestacks but we had already told the Lord that we would not argue. Whatever He had for us was good enough for our needs and wants.

Before we ever got to the place we had in mind we drove past some of my favorite beaches. I pointed to a pier and said. "This is my favorite beach in all of Southern California. My children have spent many happy hours here. We would come down from the inland whenever possible."

Betty said, "Maybe we should look for a place in this village if you like it so much.

I grinned and answered, "You dreamer. Are you aware that this is one of the most prestigious expensive areas of the West Coast? We couldn't even buy one room!"

We both saw the real estate sign at the same moment just as the light turned green. Betty said, "Shall I turn around?"

I nodded and felt my heart in my throat. Was I hearing the Lord right or did my wishful thinking deceive me? I shrugged and smiled uneasily. "We are crazy, Betty," I said, "but it doesn't cost anything to ask."

We smiled sheepishly at each other as we walked up to the door of the real estate office. Two women stood at their desks, cleaning up. Closing time was hopefully at hand for both of them. One woman hurried out so she wouldn't be delayed. The other lady looked up, holding her purse in her hand. "Can I help you?" she said pleasantly.

"I do not mean to keep you," I stuttered, embarrassed. "We are sorry to be so late but we just wondered if you have any properties below a hundred thousand dollars?" Betty gulped.

"Not really," she said with a pondering expression. "What is it you are looking for?"

Betty and I took turns giving her the needed information as fast as possible because she admitted her husband was waiting to take her to their anniversary dinner.

We urged her to leave since she obviously did not have anything suitable for us, but she insisted on staying. "How do you feel about a town house?" she asked.

"I don't think we would like it," I assured her. We didn't think that apartment living would provide enough privacy and quietness which I need for my writing....

The little saleslady dragged us nearly against our will to several places. We went with her to look because we liked her and she tried so hard to help us. The first condominium had a bar and the wrong colors. The second place was much too expensive. The sun was setting and I worried about her frustrated husband and the delayed dinner. We agreed to see one more place.

The owners of the condominium were not home. The agent fumbled with the key and finally got it unlocked. We walked in and I held my breath. I gave Betty a quick glance. If she did not like it I did not want to force her. To me, it was perfect. Glass doors opened onto a little balcony and to a magnificent view. The housing complex had been built at the edge of a golf course and we looked across to a small lake with a water fountain, hanging willows, surrounded by well-kept grassy green fairways, flowering trees and various other vegetation.

Betty looked at me and nodded. She told me later that she hoped I'd like it as much as she did. She didn't want to insist since I had expressed my dislike for condominiums.

It looked too good to be true. My head whirled. Our

saleslady said: "You have one limitation. Since this is an adult community, children cannot live here, only visit."

"That is not our problem," I smiled, "my baby just went away to college. But can we afford such a place?"

She quoted the price. It was well below the hundred thousand dollars Betty was so concerned with.

The place had not even been officially listed for sale yet. Two retired ladies decided to sell because several steps led to the entrance and one of them had just suffered a heart attack. So they wanted to buy another place without steps to climb.

My thoughts raced. We had to pay twenty percent down. I figured fast. If we scraped every available penny together we might be able to do it. Our combined incomes could make the mortgage payments. But I had to make sure that this was the Lord's choice for us. I decided to lay out one last fleece. I said to the saleslady, "Would you contact the owners and tell them we are making a counter offer?" I quoted a price five thousand dollars lower than they had asked for. "And," I said, "could they leave the washer, dryer and all the kitchen equipment, including the refrigerator?"

Betty gulped again and I did not know why. She told me later that I had demanded the impossible. She had worked once in an escrow office and realized I was demanding too much of a bargain.

The sales woman took our earnest money and could finally leave for her dinner. We stayed in a motel nearby because she wanted to contact the ladies the next morning and let us know immediately.

Betty and I had a restless night. I would wake up and ask the Lord worried questions. "Lord," I prayed, "if this goes through we are deeply in debt. Is this right for us?"

"I can take care of it," He assured me.

"The interest rates sound very high to me," I continued.

"They will not appear high at all in a few years," the Lord reassured me.

"Jesus," I wondered next. "Will we qualify for a loan? I have no credit, Betty will have to carry it all."

"I can handle it well, trust Me," the Lord comforted me over and over.

We stayed close to the telephone all morning. When the call came, Betty answered. My mouth felt too dry to talk.

"Congratulations," the agent said, "you are the proud owners of a beautiful condominium at the golf course. The ladies accepted your counter offer. I will come and pick you up so you can meet them and sign some papers."

We met them and liked them as well as their home. I told them that we had prayed to find the right place. The woman with the recent heart attack said, "We prayed that if it was God's will to sell, He would send us a buyer. He obviously has because you came before it even went officially on the market." All four of us knew that the whole deal was right and God has His hand in everything.

By Saturday noon we were ready to return home and tell Tim. I looked at Betty. "Do you know that we just bought a place and we have no idea where a grocery store or bank is? We better drive around and orient ourselves to our new surroundings."

We quickly investigated the area. To our great relief we found out that we were close enough to civilization to shop and run errands without losing too much time. The market was only a mile away.

On our way home I wondered what Tim would say. He and I often didn't see eye to eye on important matters.

I shall never forget the talk we had when I announced that I would resign as a master teacher and go full-time into speaking and writing. I was already alone and needed my big, steady salary to pay for my children's education. I had three in private schools and Tim would occasionally need some help for extra bills and insurance.

I did not resign without a struggle. I felt like Simon
Peter stepping out on the water. It made little sense to
give up all my earthly security, except I believed that
the Lord had told me to do so.

Tim looked up at me and shook his head in utter
bewilderment when I told him. "Mother," he reasoned,
are you using your head at all in this? You know how
many unemployed teachers are walking the streets
right now. And you are throwing away a secure,
respected position without being forced to do so? If they
fired you or had you laid off it would be different. But
you are resigning by your free choice. Use your head,
Mother. The kids need you for several more years to
come. Peter is only fourteen years old."

"I know, Tim," I had answered, feeling helpless to
explain it sensibly. "I fully understand what you are
saying and I appreciate your concern. But I cannot go
by my head, son, I have to go by my heart and by what
God shows me. You see, Christians cannot lean on their
own understanding, they must first obey God."

"Are you *sure* God wants you to do this?" Tim had
persisted.

"I am sure," I answered, "I am very sure." I wasn't
quite as sure as I sounded and I went back to God again
and again for confirmation. Of course, looking back
now I know for *sure* it was God's will and the right
decision I made then.

Tim also questioned my wisdom when I leased our
present home. It had to be painted, fixed up, debugged,
and I put much elbow grease and my whole vacation
into the clean-up. But now he seems to like the place
well enough that he is in no hurry to move away.

Well, I began to prepare myself for another difference
of opinion. I knew it would sound presumptuous to
announce: "Guess what? We went out to look for a
house and we found one and bought it in less than two
hours. We didn't look around too much. We walked in
and knew that was it. Come and see it."

But that is exactly what I said and Tim gave me one

of his famous looks. I called the two ladies and asked if
we could show the place to my son. We drove down and
walked in. Tim checked things thoroughly, even some
of the faucets, and found everything in top condition.
He stood deep in thought on the balcony and admired
the scenery.

On the way home I waited for his comments. He
turned to me and said, "You never cease to amaze me,
Mother. Are you actually aware of what you two just
did?"

I shook my head. No, I didn't have any idea. Did we
risk too much? Was the debt unreasonable? Could it be
a bad investment and Betty would lose all her money? I
braced myself for the arguments.

Tim said, "You bought yourself the home most people
dream of but never find. It's the 'in thing' to live on a
golf course, Mom, but you wouldn't know that." He
shook his head. "How can two little ladies walk in
without looking and find the bargain of a lifetime? The
area is just beginning to develop and so prestigious it
should not only be good living but a great investment.
How did you manage to do so well in such a short time?"

I smiled and gave him a long look, too. He knew my
thinking. He continued, "OK, Mom, I have to admit
something: things *do* work for you. I must agree that
you did fine after you resigned. The house you leased
turned out to be a good place to live over the last years.
You are doing something very few people have dared to
do with their lives. You are doing what you like best.
Now, you even found the perfect home. I have to hand it
to you, your courage paid off."

In my heart I said, "Thank You, Jesus." Aloud I said,
"Tim, you might not believe it, but I am not the one who
brings all those things about, I just let the Lord lead."

Yes, Betty and I are letting our strong Husband
handle things more and more for us. The loan got
approved before we left for speaking tour again. Our
real estate lady assured us that she had never in her
whole career seen a credit approval come through so

quickly.

Final papers were mailed to us when we were in the Midwest. The former owners were glad to stay for a few more weeks because their next house was not finished. We ordered a big penthouse couch as soon as our loan was approved and it was delivered shortly before we returned home for the Thanksgiving weekend.

The two ladies will never know how much it meant to us that they left the place in spotless condition when they moved out. Even the windows were washed and every cupboard cleaned. We moved on Thanksgiving weekend and quickly settled in. Tim will keep the other house for a while longer, so we did not have to move a four-bedroom house all at once. We can store stuff or give it away without time pressure. It will take weeks to unpack all our books. We plan to line the hallway with bookcases. I am so glad we have the next few weeks free. Betty and I have some special ideas to make the place uniquely ours, and it will take time. For right now I am content just to curl up on our new couch and marvel. I feel like I am dreaming.

"Lord," I overflow in my heart, "we had prepared ourselves to live in a little cracker box. Instead we live like royalty. We even have landscapers and gardeners to take care of our surroundings. I have the beach and the greenery of the mountains all in one setting. I would not have known how to ask for it because I did not know it existed. You gave us more than we dared to dream or ask for. How can we thank You enough?"

"I told you that heaven has much to give to those who give Me all. I do give it back a hundredfold and I have much more for you, just trust Me," the Lord answered lovingly.

"Lord, what more could I ask for? I am a blessed, content woman — and Betty feels the same, I am sure!"

May/*Friday Night*

I am expecting the children for a belated Mother's Day
weekend. Betty and I were still on the road on Mother's
Day and couldn't celebrate. I had to settle for some
phone conversations instead. Tim has moved into his
own apartment. Peter has settled surprisingly well into
his new dormitory life and seems to enjoy what he is
doing. The girls are in the final spurts toward graduation next year.

Since last fall Betty and I have traveled in a motor
home across the land. We hoped it would make our long
trips easier when we can use our own cooking facilities.
It also saves motel bills. We had no idea what it
entailed, though Betty approached the idea cautiously.
She knew she would have to do all the driving since I do
not feel qualified. Neither of us had ever driven a large
vehicle, but she is a very secure, experienced driver. She
was an all-American kid who has driven since her
teenage years. I learned to drive less than ten years ago.

I shall never forget our first trip last fall. Betty had
told the Lord over and over again that He would have to
drive, she could only hold the steering wheel. We had a
few close calls. Once we had to go up a steep winding
path. Both sides of the narrow road were lined with old
rough stone walls. She underestimated the width on a
sharp turn and the mini-home wedged itself securely
against one wall. I got out and directed her backup, one
inch at a time, while we both prayed and literally
soaked in sweat. All the while we backed up we heard
loud crunching sounds and wondered if the side of the
vehicle would be totally ruined by the sharp rocks or if
we would be able to travel on. When the ordeal was over
and Betty had pulled into a wide parking spot, we both
walked with shaky knees around our RV. We couldn't

believe our eyes. Not one scratch on the whole side? How could this be? We had both cringed at the grating noises. Puzzled, we walked back to inspect the wall and understood. At the place of our close encounter we found the cutting stones completely covered with a blanket of juicy ice plants, now completely crushed to green pulp. "Thank You, Lord," we both said aloud and in unison. The plants would grow again in a short time, and we drove on to the next appointment.

Betty and I are not mechanically inclined at all. If our vehicle broke down we would not even know where to start looking for the problem. We had been told that our mini-home had an electric fuel pump to help in high altitudes and over mountain passes. As we rolled for the first time up and down the Rockies we often noticed that our vehicle hesitated and almost stopped before it picked up and sputtered on again. We thought it was the fuel pump.

When we stayed at the Midwestern city where our RV was built, we went to the factory and asked for a complete tuneup and diagnostic test. The mechanic's report flustered us a bit. "How you ladies ever got over the mountains and this far I'll never know," he said with awe in his voice. "You have absolutely no bearings left in the rear. Your wheels should have locked completely at least a thousand miles ago. You could have been in deep trouble."

We nodded in silence. We are both more than aware that we could be in serious trouble every mile of our way — engine trouble, tire problems, bad weather, storms, desert winds that push high vehicles off the road, accidents — yes, we had seen several terrible wreckages on the sides of the highways, crushed and splintered. We knew about all the evils that could befall us.

I tried to explain that God drove all our vehicles and He was able to drive even without bearings. But I am not sure it made much sense to our friend. People often give us the strangest looks when we say certain things that seem rather natural to us.

Well, this spring, Betty did not feel as unprepared for our RV travel as last fall. After the first ten thousand miles she drove the big box as confidently as our small car, well, almost as confidently. She is a California driver and we began this tour by driving through snow and ice in the Midwestern states. We did not anticipate winter weather in the early spring and it took us completely by surprise.

The driving was not our single prayer concern. We not only had to be able to make it on time, we also often needed the Lord's overruling of bad weather during the meeting itself. If a blizzard hit just before a community meeting, months of preparation by an efficient committee could be wiped out. Some people think us naive because we pray about the weather, but we know better. The Bible text that informs us that Satan is the prince of the powers of the air has a new meaning for us since we have been driving across the continent twice a year. I believe that the Lord has delayed or softened many a storm just because we asked. And if it snows too much, He can make a way, literally, as we found out just a few weeks ago.

We had driven on snow-plowed, but still icy Interstate highways for most of the day and wondered how we would fare once we left the highway to get to a friend's house out in the country. We needn't have worried, we followed a snowplow right to her driveway. The next day we drove on a two-lane country road with high snowbanks on both sides. A truck with a loaded trailer pulled ahead of us up a hill. It looked like the long trailer carried several heavy telephone poles. As we watched, the load seemed to shift. Betty said, "There is something drastically wrong with that truck ahead." And just then to our unbelieving eyes the trailer became unhitched and we saw it veer off into a snowdrift while the truck continued up the road. No traffic came the other way, Betty passed both vehicles and then we had time to gulp and say, "Thank You, Jesus." I finally said to Betty. "Well, my dear, logically that heavy load should have rolled right down the hill and hit us head on. Guess who turned it into the snowbank?"

We told some of these adventures to a dear old lady we always visit in her nursing home when we get to her state. She shook her head and said, "You two ladies scare me, you seem to have a special line straight to heaven."

I laughed and assured her that *every* child of God has the same hotline to heaven. We might use it a bit more because we have no other place to go for help and wisdom.

Then there are other people who do *not* have this same attitude about our relationship with the Lord. They resent it. They even deny that it exists.

I know with deep gratitude that this ministry has many friends. Every meeting, every speaking tour adds more friends and supporters, and we thank the Lord for them. But we also have our enemies, people who oppose us, spread ugly rumors about our personal lives and question that God would be willing to protect us, or what's more, use us!

It never ceases to amaze me what evangelicals can do to each other in the name of Christ. The longer I travel the more I wonder.

I cannot think of any other time when a person needs more help and support than when a home breaks up, either through death or divorce. The latter seems to be worse because when death takes a spouse, the grieving person gets a little sympathy at least for a short time; then later the bereaved has to adjust to loneliness or find a new mate. Both privileges, however, are denied to a divorced person, guilty or not.

I watched in utter astonishment as most of my many "church friends" withdrew from me and my children when the divorce took place. No minister ever came to see me, nobody called to say: "Whatever has happened, I am praying for all of you and I love you." People either took sides or stayed away. Some did more: they gossiped or condemned. I would have never believed it if I hadn't experienced it myself, but the evangelicals are perhaps the only group who shoot their own wounded. Denominations have different distinctives and are very proud of them, but there are a few things most groups agree on. On the positive side they agree on the diety of Jesus Christ; and on the negative, most church people agree that there are two unpardonable sins — the sin against the Holy Spirit, and divorce. (The first one is "debatable," the second is not.) Divorce is clearcut; it's wrong and, like lepers, those who get one must leave the camp. I watched myself being kicked out of my church camp. Members in good standing who didn't know me felt called to write and condemn or advise me.

Now, from the very beginning we have received much mail in our young organization and most letters delight my heart. People thank me for my books, tell me their problems, and ask for prayer or help. I often say, like Corrie ten Boom, that such letters or compliments are like flowers. I gather them in a bouquet and hand them to Jesus. Either a few flowers or a large bundle can make a beautiful arrangement, but it takes a single stone to make a person bleed. One cruel remark or letter can wipe out the glow of many kind words for a long time. I have struggled through days of deepest depression in the past, just because someone felt called to show me the "only right way." Some church saints don't know too much about the love of God but they know there are only two ways: theirs and the wrong way.

From the beginning the Lord has encouraged me not to defend myself. Every time I felt I had to react, I was sorry. Nobody knows another person's heart, only God does. If things are right between the Lord and us as children of God, He will defend us, we don't have to. If we have sin in our hearts or lives, Jesus has to show it to us. I shall never understand why Christians so often "grade" sin. Why do we excuse judging, gossip, backbiting, and slander, but family problems are always unforgiveable? I have seen capable, dedicated ministers lose their jobs because their wives left them. I have watched how a church board stripped a church organist of her job because someone started a rumor about her and her roommate. She ended up lonely and crushed.

What can a single person do and not come under suspicion? Because Betty never married some people wonder what is wrong with her. If I were to be seen in male company, I would be questioned about my morals. Since I travel with another single woman some people insist we must be having a problem. Is every single person condemned to complete isolation just to please some wagging tongues?

I shall never forget the time when a minister of my former church approached me. Betty and I had just finished a weekend seminar, sponsored by the ministerial association in a North Dakota town. The man had attended two of the three daylong sessions. He sat in the first row, his church affiliation prominently printed on his name tag. He listened intently and made many notes. He sat through two hours of questions and answers the people had requested. At the end of the seminar he asked if he could talk to me in private. Betty looked concerned. She has seen people like him tear me to pieces before. I told her not to worry, Jesus would take care of me.

The man sounded sincere and embarrassed. He squirmed. "Are you aware of the gossip that surrounds you?" he asked.

"Which gossip," I smiled, "there have been so many."

"Well," he continued, "people claim you left your husband for a woman."

I looked at him and said, "Can I answer with another question?" He nodded. "How did you enjoy Betty's Bible teaching?" I asked.

His eyes lit up. "She is an excellent teacher and a fine scholar. I made many notes. I have to admit, I learned a lot."

"Do you believe that God used her in this seminar to show the people more about the Bible and Jesus?" I asked quickly.

"Oh, yes," the minister agreed. "No doubt about it, and the response was most enthusiastic. The people didn't want to leave."

I looked straight into his eyes. "Brother," I said, "do you think God would use Betty the way He does if there was sin in her life? If you think I can't be trusted, could you at least consider her record and obvious love for the Lord?"

The man looked at me in great surprise. "Of course," he said. "Of course, why didn't I think of it? How could God use you both so mightily if the rumors were true? I am sorry I asked."

I fought tears. "Look," I said, "how can a person truly defend herself? Would it really matter if I said yes or no? Don't people make up their minds and believe as they wish? The only thing I can suggest is that you pray about it. I even had to tell that to my children when the mudslinging got heavy. God is the only One who can defend us. So please go to Him for the answer."

"I got my answer," the minister said, "and please forgive me if I upset you."

We parted as friends and I waited until I got into the privacy of our motel room before I had a good cry. "Lord," I sobbed while cooling my swollen face with a wet washcloth because we had to go out to dinner, "when will these accusations stop? I am so sick and tired of it, and it is certainly not fair to Betty. She didn't even have a divorce or any such thing and now she lives, for my sake, under ugly rumors."

The Lord answered clearly, and in a firm way. "It is time you stop worrying about such things. Did the accusations ever stop Me when I walked the earth? What people say does not reflect *your* behavior but only what they think in their own minds. Remember, 'as a man thinketh, so is he.' They only show their own ideas, not yours."

I shared the Lord's words with Betty. She looked at me and said, "I always feel bad when you are attacked but I do feel more sorry for those who attack you. I am convinced that God does not take it lightly when someone tries to hurt one of God's servants. The Bible says, 'Touch not My anointed.'"

I thought about Betty's words as we traveled home. I never thought about our being anointed, but I believe she is right. Anyone who serves the Lord, guided by the Holy Spirit, is anointed. It is not a matter of theological degrees or positions. It is a question of dedication — how much any child of God is the Lord's anointed vessel. What a sobering thought! How careful all of us should be not to judge or abuse somebody's reputation. We might think of it as only a small matter, but our judging could be a very big offense to God's loving heart.

August/
Sunday at Morning Dawn

Jet lag can do strange things to a traveler. Betty and I just returned from Israel and I woke up after a few short hours, my stomach demanding a meal! This time it will take a little longer to get back to our regular schedule because we spent the whole summer in the Middle East. The Lord gave us another desire of our hearts. Betty had dreamed for many years about a chance to learn the Hebrew language in Israel. This was the summer God opened the door for it.

We led an American tour group in May through the Holy Land and parts of Europe. They flew home without us while Betty and I returned from Germany to Israel and registered for summer school.

Our *Ulpan*, as the Israelis call any of their language schools, is in Netanya, a beach city just north of Tel Aviv, and right on the Mediterranean Sea.

I felt apprehensive, out of place, deeply intimidated. I wondered how our fellow students would treat me as soon as they heard my German accent. I needn't have worried. Everybody around us talked with an accent. We had deliberately chosen a Jewish school over a western institution, which is in Jerusalem. We not only wanted to learn the language but learn to understand Jewish thinking. Betty had investigated all possibilities and found out that only one immigrants' school accepted non-Jews and tourists. We dared to apply.

The application process had been an ordeal in itself. We needed a clean bill of health, certified by a physician. We filled out pages of detailed information about our background and training and we had to provide a recommendation from two Jews or friends of Jews.

When we sent our papers away last spring I was pretty sure I would never be accepted and I had said so in my cover letter. My list of training included a Nazi youth leadership school and I had been honest about it. I did not feel right about flying under false colors and I wrote: "If you don't want me in your school, I understand fully, and I will love you anyway!"

When the letters of acceptance arrived I could not believe my eyes. I was plainly scared and talked a lot to the Lord about it. He assured me and calmed the butterflies in my stomach. I know myself so well. I react strongly to people's rejection by withdrawing into a shell. I also know my memory handicap. I have carried it ever since my young years when I escaped from a Communist labor camp. Once I suffered through a period of time when I couldn't even remember my foster mother's name. I still have a problem today remembering some names, numbers, dates — so how would I be able to learn a new language in one summer?

Well, I didn't, but I had a wonderful time trying to cooperate with the teacher. Betty did the real studying. She is a born scholar and took the work seriously. I accused her of being teacher's pet but she disagreed. While Betty studied Hebrew, I watched the people. We started in the *kita alef* class. That means "dumbbell" in my vocabulary, and is for those who don't know a single Hebrew word. I felt advanced because I could say *toda* when we started and also *boker tov*. Our Jewish guide had taught us to say "thank you" and "morning good" while we toured Israel.

There is a difference between being a tourist in Israel or a fellow student in a Jewish school, we found out fast. The Israelis cater tremendously to any visitor since tourism is their number two industry and an important source of their national income, Jews treat Jews much rougher, we discovered. And we were treated like fellow Jews.

We had one of the best teachers we could have asked for. Her name was Zmira (which means nightingale)

and could she ever sing and dance! But she did not
make music in class. Her no-nonsense approach overwhelmed me in the beginning. In a class of around
twenty students, an English diplomat, Betty, and I
were the only non-Jews. The rest were immigrants who
had to learn Hebrew as fast as possible in order to
survive and integrate. For their sake, Zmira hammered
away at us — up to eight hours a day, six days a week,
and she made us repeat phrases over and over until she
thought we had gotten them.

For the first time it dawned on me what a miracle had
taken place in order to create a Hebrew-speaking Israel
within the last few decades. The students in our class
alone were from at least ten different countries, speaking *only* Russian, Polish, Swedish, Dutch, Portuguese,
English, Danish, French or Spanish when they arrived.
Zmira spoke just about every one of those languages
and gave us all the translation help we so desperately
needed — for the first two weeks. Then she announced
that we could not use any other language but Hebrew in
her class. I groaned and Betty smiled. When I got back
in our room, I asked Betty to write down in English
letters the Hebrew words for, "I don't know." She wrote,
"Ani lo yodat." I practiced the words until I could say
them fluently. They became my most used words in the
weeks to follow. Zmira would laughingly shake her
head and say in exasperation: "Oh, Maria, Maria!" I
did not go by the name of Hansi in the Ulpan. I did not
say too much about myself or my background at all.
Both of us tried to listen and observe and loved every
moment of it. Betty and I love Israel and the Jewish
people.

They might have never known much about us if I had
had my way. But the Lord overruled. I had gotten
acquainted with a German Christian nurse. She wanted to work in the *Hadassah* hospital in Jerusalem but
could not go on duty unless she first had a basic hold of
the Hebrew language. She attended an advanced class.
We sat together during a lunch break and she

recognized my accent. She asked me about my background and I shared some basic facts. Next she asked what I did for a living and I told her that I was a Christian writer. I mentioned that one of my books had been translated into the German language and gave her the title. She couldn't believe the coincidence. Her mother had given her my book for Christmas and she had read it. She liked it, she said. "Do you have any other books available?" the young woman inquired eagerly.

"Not in German," I smiled.

"Oh," she said, "I read fluently in English, too."

"Well," I hesitated, "I did pack a few copies of our latest little book about the Middle East. I don't know if it would interest you. It's written from an American point of view."

She insisted and I handed her the little red book with some misgivings. The back cover announced that a former Nazi had written it.

After a few days, one of our classmates, a Jew from the USA, approached me and asked if he could have a copy of my East Wind book, too. I asked for a reason and he said he had been told by our mutual friend, the nurse, that it was an excellent book and every Jew should read it. I gave him a copy, and the demand began to grow.

About three weeks into our stay at the Ulpan, the school went on a field trip. Betty and I decided to stay behind because we had seen that particular place during our last tour and we desperately needed the time to catch up on our studies.

In the late afternoon, I suggested a walk, my head could not absorb another word. As we returned from the nearby beach, the school's founder came out of her office and called to us. Her name is Shulamit and she is the personification of a typical Jewish matron to me — short and stocky, a prominent nose, small searching eyes, brown tinted hair with outgrowing gray roots thinly covering a round head, no make-up, a plain mid-calf length dress, barefoot — and always in a whirl of activities or conferences.

We attended her morning Bible classes faithfully. These were not compulsory and very few students showed up because regular attendance cut our breakfast time severely. To us it was worth it. We were absolutely fascinated not only by her Hebrew approach but by the new insights she shared. Shulamit had been obviously impressed by Betty's Old Testament knowledge, but we had never talked at any other time. I didn't expect any personal contact after our Jewish lady said one morning in connection with a Bible lesson about the Moabites: "They are like the Germans. We have no right to ever forgive them, take them into our midst, or forget the past. It is wrong for our young generation to begin to ignore the Holocaust."

I never said a word. I didn't speak or smile too much the whole day. I ached for both of us and wondered more than ever how I got accepted into her summer program. Yes, the death of six million Jews was a terrible reality and she had every right in the world to say what she did. The only two things she did not realize were that not every German had been a part of the Nazi genocide, and that without forgiveness there would never be a healing.

I, for instance, did not know about concentration camps until the inmates had been liberated by the Allies after the war and the Third Reich had ceased to exist. When I first heard about them, I did what many Germans still do today, I refused to believe it and ignored the fact. The intolerable, horrendous truth would have crushed me if I had had to accept it all at once. It could only sink in little by little. After I became a Christian, the Lord brought it into focus through Corrie ten Boom.

Tante Corrie helped me to forgive myself for once belonging to a group of people who were capable of atrocities I couldn't even imagine. I then promised God and my own heart that I would help make up to any Jew

I met what my race had done to his. My little book on the Middle East was a beginning, because more and more of my Jewish schoolmates read it through and liked it.

When Shulamit called out to us I panicked for a moment. Did someone tell her about the back cover of my book? Would she lash out at me or even ask me to leave?

Her first words increased my apprehension. "I am mad at you," she said in her halting English and she frowned.

I swallowed hard. "What did we do?" I said and frowned back.

"You give everybody your book. How come you don't give a copy to me?" She asked with a twinkle in her eye.

I stared at her. "But, Shulamit," I stammered, "how could I know you wanted one? Have you seen the back cover? After your statement in Bible class I consider myself lucky to still be in your school."

"Yes," she said, "someone showed me that it says you have been a Nazi youth leader, but I don't believe it. You are too nice a person."

"Shulamit, it is true," I interrupted her. "I did attend a Nazi school in Prague, and furthermore, I told you honestly about it in my application papers, I even told your admissions committee that I would understand if you turned me down, and I would love you anyway."

"There is no committee," she said, "I decide who comes." A surprised look crossed her face and she continued, "How unusual. For the twenty-eight years my school has existed, this spring, for the first time, it happened that I was so busy I simply handed the whole stack of applications to my secretary and said, "Send an acceptance letter to all of them."

Betty and I looked at each other and my heart said, "Thank You, Jesus." I had to learn not to say it aloud, and that is never easy for me.

"Why did you become a Nazi?" she asked next, and her eyes clouded over.

"Shulamit," I said quietly. "I am from Czechoslovakia and was raised as an orphan by a German
peasant woman who was a Christian. Hitler made my
land part of the German Reich and I was sent by Nazi
educators to a youth leadership school. For me it
appeared to be the chance of a lifetime to make something of myself. I was the poorest kid in a remote
mountain village and slept in a hayloft.

"OK," she said with obvious relief, "You are a Czech,
not a German, and they forced you into their school."

I tried to set the record straight because I am of
Austrian German origin and nobody had to force me to
attend Nazi school. I thought I had the rainbow in both
hands when I left my little world to go to Prague. Never
had I seen a big city or any other such sophistication,
and I was thrilled.

Shulamit waved my explanations aside, they simply
did not fit her code of ethics and her Jewish frame of
reference. She liked us both and her rationalization
permitted her to do what she could not have done
otherwise. She invited us to her own home. We accepted
and I had a lump in my throat, I felt so honored.

Thanks to Betty's insights into the Hebrew culture, I
had known for some time that a Jew never invites a
person to his home unless he or she wants to be a friend.

As soon as we arrived at her place she offered us juice
and crackers. Another ingrained ancient custom, which
dates back to Old Testament times, makes eating
together not only a thoughtful gesture but a pledge of
friendship. This, we found out, is not only true for the
Israelis of today, but also for Arabs, Turks, and other
orientals. The Eastern world considers food sacred
enough that sharing it symbolizes trust and loyalty
toward one another. Food can never be shared with an
enemy. Refusal of offered food suggests rejection of
intended friendship. Betty shares this important information with every tour group we take to the Middle
East. We Westerners are so ignorant of other people's
customs and culture and are not even aware how deeply

we can offend someone by our flippant "no-thank-you-I'm-on-a-diet" answer.

We, of course, accepted Shulamit's refreshments gladly and while I sipped my orange juice, we talked. I gave her an autographed copy of our little red book and tried to answer her rapid-fire questions. She could not talk fast enough; it seemed like a dam had broken in her troubled soul. She came from one of the leading orthodox families of Israel, her relatives included a former Israeli president and a brother who is at present one of the high government leaders. She and Mr. Begin belonged to the same historic group which was blended together by underground resistance, suffering agony, triumph, defeat, and victory for the young state of Israel. Her whole life revolves around one center only: The future of her beloved *Eretz Yisrael* and the coming of the Jewish Messiah.

When she paused for breath I interrupted her with a question: "Shulamit, I know that you and your people suffered terribly, but can there ever be a healing? I ache for both races. The German nation carries the burden of collective guilt; the Jews carry the awful burden of collective hate. Can we ever forgive, forget, and heal? The key to any healing is forgiveness."

She gave me the look of an eagle with broken wings when she said, "We can *never* forget or forgive. If we do, it could happen again. We must remember — always! We can accept individuals, like Ruth in the Bible who came as a Moabitess and became one of us, or you who are a true friend of Israel now; but we can *never* forgive the German nation. We betray the millions of Jews who died."

Never in all my life have I longed to share the "new" covenant and the love of my Lord Jesus with anybody more than with Shulamit, my Jewish friend. Never have I felt more helpless, humble, and unable to do so. I looked at her and understood suddenly the words of the Apostle Paul in his letters to the Corinthians and to the Romans. These precious people carry a veil over their

hearts and inner eyes, and it is partially for my sake, so
that I, as a Gentile, may be grafted into the spiritual
Israel. I knew that I could never preach to her, I
represent a double-veil. My race brought on the Holocaust. In the name of Christianity, the Jews went
through the Inquisition, the Crusader attacks; even
Adolph Hitler claimed to be a Roman Catholic. For an
orthodox Jew who still believes in the Mosaic principle
of "an eye for an eye, a tooth for a tooth, and a life for a
life," the words *German* and *Christian* have to be curse
words.

I understood, and I knew I had only one gift to give: I
can love them. I said so to Shulamit and she tried very
hard not to get emotional. Jews pride themselves on
their tough exterior.

When we started to leave so that we would be on time
for our evening meal at the Ulpan, Shulamit did the
unexpected: "Stay for supper," she said with a smile. "I
have not much in the cupboard because I am never
home, but we can find some ingredients to make a good
soup."

Betty and I gave each other a quick glance and both
swallowed hard. It is one thing to share refreshments,
but to take part in a meal is the show of ultimate
friendship. We knew that in an orthodox home the meal
begins with the head of the house reaching for a basket
of dry bread slices. He or she breaks the bread in pieces
and hands it to everyone at the table. Betty set the table,
orthodox style. She never touched the bread basket. We
waited and wondered. Would Shulamit go so far as to
break bread with us? She did! And I fought tears while I
swallowed the piece of dry bread she handed to me. It
wasn't hard to love her — and all her sincere
Jewishness.

We became like sisters in the weeks that followed.
Nobody taught us more about Hebrew thinking and
living than Shulamit. Her Bible lessons invigorated us
but it was her own philosophy of life that showed us the
special place God's chosen people have in our world.

Hebrews think in pictures, they always have, ever since they became a nation at the foot of Mount Sinai. God told them not to make visible images, so they turned to word pictures. The whole Old Testament is a big picture book. Even the Lord Jesus taught in parables and a parable conveys one great concept in a tangible illustration. Jews haven't changed. They still communicate in pictures.

Shulamit came flying into our room one day. She had just called a high government official in Jerusalem. She shared the conversation and then said, "You know I have to be careful in what I say. This is a man's world and I am a woman. I must walk between the raindrops and not get wet."

Another time I asked her, "Why did you start a school like this? This language school is the only Jewish place where non-Jews are allowed to come and study. I know that you have been criticized for it."

She cocked her head in her typical fashion and thought for a moment. Then she said, "I did not do it because I am very smart or clever, but I am absent-minded, I forgot to lock my heart."

"Bless you, precious lady," I thought. "You didn't lock your heart toward us two Christian Gentile women either, and God will bless you for it."

The Lord did bless her in a special way during the time we spent at the Ulpan. We did a lot of praying, that's for sure, because we couldn't talk to her about our Lord, but she must have sensed His presence.

She looked at us one day and said, "So many good things have happened here since you came. I wonder why?"

I looked straight into her dark eyes and said, "Do you really want to know?"

She hesitated, "Well, yes..."

I said, "Shulamit, Betty and I believe in the God of Abraham, Isaac and Jacob, just as you do. We pray much to the Holy One that He might hold down the power of the evil one who causes great problems for you, the school, and all of Israel."

"Please, keep on praying," she said eagerly. "This place needs your prayers."

The most touching moment came just before our graduation day. After that we had to fly back to California. Shulamit came into our room and sat on the only chair that fit between our two cots. She appeared solemn when she announced, "I have an offer for you two. I am willing to give you both a year-long scholarship at the Ulpan. We will pay tuition and living expenses if you will help out between classes in the office with our English correspondence."

Betty and I were speechless. When I finally found my voice, I said, "We are greatly honored, my friend, but we cannot do it. Much work and a speaking tour are waiting for us at home. But why do you offer such a generous gift to us?"

"I want to keep you here because we need your prayers," she said wistfully. "What will happen when you leave?"

"We can pray even on the other side of the ocean," I reassured her, but she couldn't see it our way.

She spread her arms across our backs when we said goodbye to her, and I shall never forget her final words: "Don't forget to pray, will you? You people seem to have a special line to God which we don't have." Her voice trailed off and she ran to talk to others. She never looked back at us and I understood.

A former member of the Israeli underground does not cry when two Christian Gentile students leave. But I allowed myself to do so.

I cried when I hugged Zmira and the many other Jewish people who had become our friends. I still cry sometimes when I remember them and when I pray for them and their land. "Pray for the peace of Jerusalem: they shall prosper that love thee," my Bible says (Psalm 122:6). Yes, and we shall pray until the veils are lifted! I can't wait to see that day when Israel will be permitted to forgive and heal and to see their long-awaited Messiah. I would love to see Shulamit's face when she finds out that her and my Messiah are the same person: Jesus our Lord. Oh, Father God, may it be soon!

November/*The Day Before Thanksgiving*

What a long and hard fall tour, and what victories our Lord has brought about. It is good to be back in our little condo for a change and it is as beautiful as we remembered it. To think that we moved in a year ago and we have only lived in it for a few weeks at a time, perhaps not more than seven weeks altogether throughout the whole year.

We had some rough times lately. I wasn't really surprised. After the great successful summer we had, the devil would try doubly hard to steal the blessing. We warn people sometimes at the end of a seminar or retreat that a mountaintop experience is often followed by a great letdown. We came back from Israel walking on air. We landed hard on rocky ground.

Our first four primary speaking appointments this fall were four weekend retreats in the Midwest, all planned by the same women's organization of a leading Protestant denomination.

I had to conquer many negative emotions before I could go and serve. It was the same group who several years ago, had canceled me with a very rude letter. At that time my marriage was in the process of breaking up and I still held high hopes that the breach could be mended. I had just resigned as a teacher and stepped out by faith into a full-time ministry of speaking and writing.

The staff of my new organization consisted of my secretary, Mary, a frail little woman, and myself. We had rented a little place in the mountains and made one room of the house our new office. I shall never forget the wording of the cancellation letter we received: "We have been informed that Hansi is in the middle of family problems. Under those circumstances we do not believe that she has *anything* to offer to our women."

Will the writer of the letter ever know how deeply she cut? For days I walked in a daze. That the Lord in His compassionate love eased the pain by giving me almost immediately other appointments in its place goes to His credit and glory. But such memories heal very slowly, I never defended myself to them, I forgave; but my soul's deep scars remained tender to the touch.

Betty received an invitation to speak for that particular group a year ago. She informed them that she had changed jobs and was now working with me. If they wanted her as a speaker they would have to invite us both. She didn't hear for a long time but finally the invitation came through — for both of us! We accepted and began to pray for the right attitude. It was not the first time I had to pray away a chip on my shoulder, but this amounted to a full-fledged battle.

We walked into the opening meeting with great misgivings. The staff sat in the first row with expressionless faces. Then I looked into a sea of faces behind them, hundreds of women's faces, smiling, tired, and expectantly waiting, and my reservations rolled away. We had come to serve, not to nurse hurt feelings!

Betty and I gave it all we had to give and by the end of the first retreat we watched a grateful audience give us a standing ovation, and the staff had smiling faces, too.

By the fourth retreat weekend we had served more than a thousand women, and the staff people were our personal friends. Some of them finally leveled with us. The woman who had written the cruel letter had moved away. At the present time the poor lady is watching her daughter go through a messy divorce. I wonder what such a mother does when her child commits "the unpardonable sin" because her husband leaves? I can't help but ache for all of them. Next we were told what happened when Betty's reply came to headquarters. It nearly shook up the whole denomination, until one of the church leaders suggested that they stop the whole nonsense and give us both a try.

"Can I ask what the true problem is?" I finally ventured.

"Well," a former president of the organization said, "I'll level with you. We have *one* minister in our denomination who fights you bitterly."

"Why?" I asked aghast. I didn't even remember his name, although I do remember that I once spoke in his church. Betty had spoken there too, but years before I had been invited. Nobody could give us a reason why the man acted so hostile toward us. I went to the Lord.

I know what the Lord showed me is true, I am sorry that things have to be that way — and it's done in the name of the Lord. Jesus showed me that there are several reasons why some people turn so antagonistic, not only toward us, but also toward others who do not meet their ideal of perfection.

People who are bound by legalism or any other prejudice are prone to lash out blindly, zealously, and with great self-righteousness. They don't do it to be malicious, they think that they do God a favor. After all, someone has to defend the purity of the faith. On the other hand, isn't it God's will that we stand up for the right and be counted?

Yes, there are times to stand firm, but never to fight. God always does that for us. All we are called to do is put on God's armor with prayer, God will do the rest.

If God's servants could learn to spend as much time in prayer as they use to argue or "defend the faith" in their own strength, many conflicts in the church communities could be avoided. I am the first one to know that a person can believe something very strongly and sincerely and still be dead wrong. I did so as a Nazi. It is very hard to admit that we can be wrong. And that is the next reason why so many difficulties plague our churches. The Western world is a man's world, and thanks to Hollywood and other strong influences, a man is taught from babyhood on that he must be tough, strong, *the* best, always right, never second, first in everything. And he must be able to handle the impossible, like John Wayne. Is it a wonder that the "male ego" becomes so defensive, over-sensitive, and so easily filled with a fear of failure?

All over this nation are pastors who try to lead out in their churches, doing their very best, but it never seems good enough. Someone else always has his church fuller, a bigger TV program, a better known name in the community. It takes a very secure, well-adjusted person to let two little women like Betty and me come in and rejoice with us when the Lord fills the church and the people enjoy our messages. Thank God, most pastors are big enough at heart and we have many clergy friends around the world. But once in a while we face fierce opposition. It is not always the pastor either, it can be his wife, a church secretary, or one lone board member. I am always surprised when I observe what *one* negative person can do. The greatest tragedy is that so often these "fighting fundies" do not even know how much damage they produce. They fight innocently, ignorantly, pleased with themselves; but nobody else can please them, for sure!

Another syndrome Betty and I have to deal with sometimes is what I call "the god syndrome." Some gentlemen don't have a problem with poor self-esteem, they know that they are God's answer to every problem on this earth. They are "the best" in every area, a little god, and they treat us earthlings accordingly. They never worry about other people's feelings either, and women don't even have feelings. In their eyes females are not human or intelligent enough to hurt or understand.

I have said it often in the last few years, and no doubt I'll say it again in the future: I understand slowly but surely why God calls more and more women to be leaders in the evangelical world. In some ministries, like ours for instance, a male ego could never survive. Americans are seldom heartless, but can they ever be thoughtless with each other. And Christians so often have the edge on it. Since we all belong to the same family of God we are apt to step on each other's toes even when we are careful. And sometimes we don't even try to be thoughtful. Pastors, leaders, presidents of institutions, doctors, teachers, principals, and other assorted professionals can so easily get into the habit of giving orders that they sometimes forget how people under them can get hurt by their unfeeling ways.

I shall never forget the time when I had finished a conference in the Midwest. It was before Betty traveled with me. I was looking forward to a full rest day. A college president called late that night. He was in a tight spot, he said, because a speaker had canceled on him forty-eight hours before a big patriotic rally on their football field. The meeting had been advertised on TV, radio and with big posters all over the city. Someone had just heard me speak at a Bible conference and brought him my message on tape. He had listened and couldn't find anything objectionable on it. Would I consider filling in?

I told him I would pray about it and call him in the morning. The Lord told me to accept, but forewarned me not to be surprised if things didn't go the way I anticipated.

I met the man in his office just before we had to go out to the football field, packed with thousands of people. He checked me sternly from head to toe and said, "Your secretary is putting up a sales table with your books and tapes. I do not think she will sell anything, our people will not touch your books. I noticed that you have a foreword by Corrie ten Boom in one of them. We don't believe in her teachings, she sides with the charismatics."

Next, the president bit his lip and said, "I haven't told anybody that you will speak in Mr. X's place. I have to introduce you now to my college board." We walked out to a circle of men in black suits, white shirts, and black ties, waiting, and the disaster was announced. If icy stares could have killed I would never have lived long enough to give the message. By then the Lord had given me my sense of humor back and I tried hard to keep my face in the proper sober setting.

It got harder when the president stepped up to the microphone. He kept me hidden from the public until the last moment. He said with a mourner's voice, "There are moments in a president's life when he does not want to be around. This is one of those moments. I am sorry to announce that Mr. X, our honored speaker, will not be with us. He canceled a few hours ago. I had no choice but to ask Hansi to take his place. All I can do is apologize to you. It looks as if we used Mr. X's name to bring you here; but believe me, please, it is as I said. All I can ask you is to forgive us for that misfortune and please, welcome Hansi anyway."

The audience welcomed me when I stepped smiling to the microphone. They did more than that. They stood up and clapped and whistled before I ever said my first word. What the college president didn't know was that I had many friends in his city and God had brought a host of them to the rally. I didn't know it either until that moment and their long standing ovation gave me a chance to wipe my eyes, catch my composure and speak — as unto the Lord. My Jesus and I got another standing ovation at the end of the speech. The people bought books and tapes like hot cakes and I heard the president say to one of his board members, "Well, we pulled out of this disaster, and came out OK."

I shall forever wonder if a male speaker could have taken that president's tactlessness and been able to speak freely. I was able to do it because I know who I am and who my Husband and Protector is.

As I said before, this kind of happening is not the usual, but the exceptional. The Lord knows how much even a woman can take!

Betty and I had some wonderful meetings in many places on this most recent tour. The reason I remember it as a rough tour is that the first and the last stops were spoiled by the same judgmental spirit.

On our way home we stayed over for one last weekend seminar in the South. Several churches had worked together for over a year to prepare for a city-wide seminar, sponsored by the Ministrial Association. Excitement seemed to run high and Betty and I looked forward to the engagement because we would be among friends. We had spoken before in the church where the meetings were to be held.

We knew something was wrong when we met with the chairman of the committee. "I don't know how many will come," she said and looked defeated. "We have one woman in this church who has fought your coming and she hasn't given up yet. She even went before the Ministrial Association demanding your cancellation. She is saying ugly things about both of you."

My heart sank. I felt too tired after nine weeks of travel to face another battle with a well-meaning defender of her faithful prejudices. I needed a lift. Near the city was a Christian commune where evangelical women had begun a work for the Lord and I have been friends with the leaders or " sisters" as they called themselves. I decided I would go and visit them between meetings to get a lift for my spirit. I wondered why the woman who drove us around gave me such a strange look when I requested it.

I didn't get to them as soon as I had hoped. The weekend meetings had been well-attended after all and the committee people smiled again. I could sense an undercurrent of resistance, however, but we prayed much and did our best. Before the last evening meeting, a patriotic community rally, I insisted on a quick trip to the commune.

I soon wished I hadn't. The leading "sister" requested a walk alone with me. Betty looked alarmed. "Don't worry," I whispered, "they are my friends."

I was aware that this particular women's group over-emphasized two facets of the Christian life: repentance and speaking the truth in love. It had always bothered me that they talked mostly about these two things as the key to God's heart and to one another. But I have learned to accept people who go to extremes. It is hard for any person to stay balanced. We Christians are no exception. Even denominations can sometimes lean off center and proudly proclaim their individual distinctives as the center of their teachings. In truth, there is only one center: Jesus Christ. And He alone is the way the truth, the doctrine, and the only key to God's heart. His love draws us together.

It was not His love that I got on our walk through their garden. It was one of the harshest lectures I have ever received. I was a sinner who had failed to repent properly or my home would not have broken up. It was all my fault because I had traveled too much and left my husband alone. I needed to stop my public ministry, repent properly and return to my husband.

"He has remarried," I said quietly.

So I had to consider it as my punishment, I was informed, and stay alone in total seclusion and complete repentance, not in public service.

I stayed calm. At the end I said, "Can I ask you a question? Suppose everything you said was true, which it is not, and that the divorce was my fault, is it possible that God could forgive me and use me anyhow?"

"Absolutely not," I was assured. God would never use an erring person like me.

I thanked the "sister" and told her I would pray about it. As an afterthought I said, "Do you know a Mrs. Y?"

"We surely do," she answered, "she comes here often to worship with us. We encouraged her to do all she could to stop your coming. You are doing a disservice to our area."

I could not find one trace of my sense of humor to pull me through that particular afternoon. In the car I told what had happened and cried. Our hostess said, "Hansi, in a way it is of the Lord that you visited them, because we would not have had the courage to tell you who really fought you. We knew how highly you regarded

them. All I can say is that we don't see it their way at
all."

The evening rally was a victory for the Lord. The
place was packed. The Spirit of God opened hearts and
purses and the tour ended in a blaze of glory.

Jesus laid some special healing on my raw wound
after the meeting. A little lady, tears rolling down her
face, came to me and asked if I could see her alone for a
moment. We walked back into the darkened empty
meeting place and she said, "I am Mrs. Y. I am the one
who fought you so hard. A committee member called me
this afternoon and pleaded with me to come and hear
you just once. I came to prove my point. God has been
dealing with me through the entire meeting. I was
wrong, Hansi; God *is* using you. Can you please forgive
me?"

We both had a good cry and we prayed together before
we parted, as friends. It wasn't hard to forgive her. She
had been so sincere in her crusade for the "sisters" that
she had forgotten that God is big enough to bring
beauty out of any ashes, even a new ministry for His
glory.

* * * * * * * *

Now I shall put the writing pad aside and store Hansi
and her speaking clothes in the closet for a while. It's
time to reach for my kitchen apron and become Mommy
for a few days. The children will soon be here, and I
know what they hope to find in our home: a smile,
harmony and peace, German food and music, good-
natured teasing and laughter — and the presence of the
Lord. They know that Jesus is the Head of this house
and they like it. They have told me so.

Tim is bringing a new girl friend. I wonder if I hear
wedding bells? What a good life I have! Thank You,
Jesus! May all thanksgiving go only to You alone —
anywhere, any place, any time.

NEW YEAR'S EVE   81

New Year's Eve/
Wednesday

It is hard to believe that more than a year has passed since I found time to write some more in this diary. Every year seems to get fuller and busier, and we spend less time than ever in our own home.

We just returned from the South yesterday. I guessed right last year when I expected wedding bells. Tim married a lovely girl from a southern state and they had a tender, beautiful wedding in a little gospel church the day before yesterday. I pointed out to him that he might not have found her if he hadn't stayed near us. God rewarded him for his unselfish decision. Both had accepted jobs in their own fields here in Southern California and a mutual friend introduced them to each other.

It seems like an unreal, sweet dream to me. The conflicts with Tim are behind me like past nightmares. I can't even picture the rebellious teenager anymore, only the beautiful wedding ceremony and Tim's radiant face when he said, "I do, forever." A minister of the gospel married them.

Of course, I sat there and cried with joy. My ever-ready tears roll often anyway, but when I am as tired as I feel right now, I can cry without a reason.

This last year took every ounce of energy out of Betty and me. We seemed to be forever on the road and in meetings all over the country. In the summer we took the largest group we ever had to Israel and Europe.

My two daughters came along and had a great time. Cathy didn't graduate until Christmas but had come near enough to the goal that both could enjoy their graduation gift of travel together.

To think that four of my five children are already through college. If the last one sticks it out to graduation I won't know how to behave. What will I do with all the money I save? No more frantic phone calls before finals, no more broken-down cars, no more worries about grade point averages!

I must give my children credit for hard work and effort. They all worked through high school and college years and paid most of their bills themselves. There was no other way, I simply don't have the income to pay it all. But even if I were rich, I would have insisted on a work-study program toward their degrees. I believe that young people appreciate anything more if they have to work for it, no matter what the object is.

I admire America's way of life greatly, but if I were asked where I see flaws, I would point first of all to the general tendency to make it too easy for the younger generation. American history seems to bear out that, ever since the arrival of the Mayflower, every generation had one great desire: to improve the lot of their children. After two hundred years we have arrived at the point where too many youngsters get every wish fulfilled. Education is served on a silver platter and many parents sacrifice every penny to see their children enjoy what the older generation only dreamed of all their hardworking lives.

This philosophy is not only destructive for families and their offspring, it could be the beginning of the end for our free way of life in America. Young people were never made to live pampered lives, no more so than young birds are supposed to remain in the nest to be fed worms by their parents for as long as the nestlings choose or wish. Adult birds have sometimes more common sense than humans do. They force their youngsters to leave the nest and teach them to fly and to feed themselves.

As I have said so often, young people need a challenge. If we protect them too much and give them "fun only," they will create their own challenge. They love to dare, and often dare for the wrong cause or a new experience. They will take what is given to them and not even appreciate the giver. They will also take for granted what America offers.

If I could sum up this last year, I would have to say that Betty and I poured our souls out before numerous audiences, reminding our fellow Americans of two main principles: America needs another mighty prayer revival, and Americans need to understand and value freedom more. Our young people are not the only ones who have forgotten what a priceless gift freedom is. We, the teachers and parents, have neglected to teach them convincingly about it, because we have forgotten it ourselves.

I can by now predict the reaction of any American audience when I say: "If I approached anyone of you as a foreigner and asked 'What is freedom?' could you give me an explanation?"

I always get a startled blank stare and then an uneasy shuffle. Next, a thoughtful hush falls over the audience. I can almost hear their surprised troubled thoughts when person after person realizes that he has never given it a single thought before.

What *is* freedom? I began to ask my American neighbors that question shortly after I arrived in America while I was learning the English language. No other word puzzled, even frightened, me more than when they would speak or sing about liberty, the innate human right to be free and of being dead rather than in bondage.

I didn't know what freedom was and why it seemed so important. After I came to America, I began to learn about the Pilgrim fathers who came to Plymouth shores to begin a new life with less religious restraints. They came to America because they were looking for freedom. I didn't! I wouldn't have known what to look for. I didn't know that something called "freedom" existed. I simply came for a better life.

My background had taught me in a harsh way that

life's first rule was silent obedient and blind conformity. One of my earliest recollections as a preschool child was the moment when I was told to do something I did not understand and I said *Warum?* (why). My foster father held his fist under my little nose and with a threatening gesture growled, "You do it because I said so, not because you understand it."

I learned very fast never to ask questions and to respond to orders with one word only: *Jawohl* (Yes, sir).

By the time I arrived in Nazi school my childhood training had prepared me to surrender in wordless obedience and blind trust to Adolph Hitler. The great tragedy of my young life and that of thousands of other young people of my generation was that we all believed we were doing the right thing. Nobody ever suggested to us that life had something more to offer than we knew or had been prepared for. Our political leadership training reinforced every principle of dictatorship. *Einer bestimmt immer* (one person gives the orders, always). We were assured it had to be so in order to keep law and order in the country, the community, the school, family, or any social group.

We were taught that Hitler was called by the Supreme Power to give the orders. A police state was needed to enforce the rules. *Das Volk* (the people) had been born into the German Reich for one reason only: to obey without questioning and to follow, if needed, into death. I not only obeyed and followed, I believed it.

Was it any wonder that the American way of life confused me in the beginning? My life in Europe had always fallen into two clear cut halves of inflexible laws. One half of my existence looked for the stiff rules that told me: *Es ist verboten* (it is forbidden). The other had tried hard to fulfill all the requirements of life under dictatorship. There was absolutely no leeway between the two structures, no room to interpret anything. It was all so clearly spelled out to the last and smallest detail.

In America I found things different. Sure, some things were forbidden, certain basic behavior required, but the American way of life permits much elbow room and respects individual interpretation in many aspects of living. People are free to think for themselves and allowed to make many decisions. After my arrival I did not know how to live with so much personal freedom and felt lost in the many non-restrictions.

The first thing I learned about freedom in a Republic was that the people *did* have it. They used it and they took it for granted. They also couldn't explain how it worked. What was there to explain? When a person is free, he or she is free to "do his own thing." That's what my helpful American neighbor answered with a smile when I asked her to define the new word for me.

Looking back I can see that she perhaps felt as perplexed as I did. She must have wondered what was bugging me. Couldn't I just be glad to live in a free country like America and let it go at that?

No, I couldn't even express myself clearly, not in the beginning. When an animal has been brought up in captivity and then is sent out to the free wilderness it can die unless it is prepared for independent survival. A caged bird comes back to the cage, frightened of all the unlimited space outside his secure structure.

The American people have been free for generations and cannot know what it entails to live without freedom. They also cannot understand that it takes time for people from other cultures and for those who have lived in political bondage to adjust to a free world.

I had so many questions and nobody was able to answer me. One matter above everything else confused me greatly. I had been taught all my life that it took *one* authority figure who had to give *every* order in any given social situation. To my surprise, in America, they didn't have a dictator or police state. They didn't even have signs everywhere that told me what I could or could not do, when authority was not around.

I sometimes share with my audiences that I even

wondered how the Americans kept the grass green in their public parks. I missed the signs I was used to from Europe: "It is forbidden to step on the grass." I still chuckle today when I remember the daring moment when, for the first time in my life, I walked off the walkway and onto the well-kept grassy area in an American city park. I wondered how soon someone would yell at me. Nobody did and I wondered next how a park could remain a park if nobody cared if people trampled the grass.

The American political system made no sense to me. The words *democracy* or *committee* or *two-party system* did not exist in my vocabulary or in my little German dictionary. I did find the word *freedom* in it, translated *Freiheit*, but that only added to my confusion. Hitler had used that word incessantly. America's freedom was different. Hitler's *Freiheit* had given me freedom *from* making decisions, *from* thinking for myself, *from* being personally responsible for my obedient behavior. Every Nazi was either free to submit to a rigid outer control of dictatorship for the good and the order of the country or lose that *Freiheit* and go to prison for breaking the rules.

I could not find the same austere outer control of public life in America, and I wondered how a country could keep law and order without a policeman at every corner. Election time boggled my mind. People dared to talk against their government? Would there be a revolution on election day? Would the country fold up in chaos and anarchy because not *one* single person took decisive control of everything?

To my astonishment I watched a country being run by many people, without any apparent central outer control, and it worked surprisingly well. What was the secret?

Since nobody seemed willing or able to explain it all to me, I went to my Lord. "This is Your dumb little kid from the hayloft again," I said, as I do so often to my Omniscient Teacher who can explain anything. "Will

You please show me how America runs? How can a country give the people so much freedom and still keep law and order? How does freedom fit into the whole system? There has to be a control somewhere to keep an organism together. A beehive runs orderly because of innate instincts in every bee, but we humans don't operate by instinct, do we?"

The Lord must have smiled. I am convinced He smiles rather often when I bring Him another one of my many perplexities of life.

He didn't answer me in one single bright flash of insight. He seldom does. Patiently He fit the puzzle together. Months became years for me in my new home-land. One day it all became clear when I read a statement by William Penn: "Men must be governed by God, or they will be ruled by tyrants."

I shall never forget the excitement that rushed through my entire being when the great truth of these inspired words struck me. I could hear inaudible bells ring and see invisible fireworks exploding. Suddenly I understood America's joy of the Fourth of July. It had become my joy, too.

America has, so far, never submitted herself to the control of a dictatorship. America's greatness lies in her inner controls. The foundation to the freedom of our nation was laid by people who not only had faith in God but were willing to be governed by the inner restraints of the Judeo-Christian ethic. Outer control can suppress the masses; inner control is always an individual decision. Freedom is a personal matter, and every American citizen either builds or undermines freedom by every choice he or she makes.

Freedom is not for everybody because a free person is willing to accept the responsibility a free life demands. Freedom is only for the courageous, and it makes good people better and bad people worse. A free person is willing to accept responsibility for his or her actions, and that was a completely new way of thinking for me. But I learned to love it. Freedom is hard to describe — it

is so intangible, but it's real. It permeates every aspect of
American life. At first I was afraid of it; then it grew on
me; now I love it. It takes second place in my life. Jesus
comes first, and He is the giver of freedom.

No wonder the devil hates it so and tries to destroy
freedom wherever he finds it. The greatest threat to
freedom is human indifference. American history showed me that people are willing to fight and even die to
keep freedom for their children. It is during times of
ease and affluence that a generation forgets the great
gift and true meaning of freedom.

Every generation must discover freedom's value, and
how it works, for themselves. That is where we parents
and teachers have failed, I believe. Many American
young people are not taught in enough detail, neither at
home nor in the school, about our Christian heritage
and the inner control that keeps freedom alive. Even
some churches fail to teach it.

My heart quivers every time I think of one of the Bible
studies Betty gives about teaching young people properly. She quotes Judges 2:7-8: "And the people served the
Lord all the days of Joshua, and all the days of the
elders that outlived Joshua, who had seen all the great
works of the Lord, that He did for Israel. And Joshua...
died." In verse 10 the great tragedy of Israel is exposed
in two simple sentences: "And also all that generation
were gathered to their fathers; and there arose another
generation after them, which knew not the Lord, nor yet
the works which He had done for Israel." The result is
tragic: "The children of Israel did evil in the sight of the
Lord" (v.11). They lost their freedom. They were greatly
distressed.

Why did the children of the new generation fail to
know the work of God? Because someone forgot to keep
the remembrance of the glorious past alive for them.
The older generation had seen it with their physical
eyes, but they forgot to pass it on as an inner vision.
They took God's work for granted and treated His
blessings as something they deserved and would have

forever. And the next generation lost it all.

I always get a knot in my stomach when Betty says: "We Christians are just *one* generation away from paganism if we forget to teach our children about the great works of the Lord. Salvation is not *inherited* from the previous generation; we need to *teach* it diligently."

I am convinced that the same is true about freedom. Unless our young people learn to treasure it as our forefathers did, they shall lose it. The blame could not be put on them but on us for failing to teach them carefully, with every precept and example.

My favorite speaking appointments are those in high schools or colleges across the nation. I have spoken in church schools and public institutions alike. In public schools I respect the laws of our land and do not "preach" Christianity, but I do inform the audience that the former Nazi youth leader has a new Master and Lord: Jesus Christ.

No matter what my assigned topic is, I always tie my urgent message about the nature of freedom into it before I close any lecture. I don't always speak about Jesus but He always speaks through and with me, no matter where I serve. And it is to His credit and glory when I say that He and I together have never lost the attention of an audience yet. Even wiggly elementary school children are willing to sit still and listen. Out of this observation the Lord gave me, one day, a simple but most effective illustration of inner control and freedom.

I had shared my life story before a large high school assembly in a gymnasium — built for sports, not for good acoustics. The sound system was ineffective and I saw some of the students strain to catch my words. To add to the misery, it was a very hot day. In spite of it the sea of young faces responded with smiles, seriousness, camaraderie, and rapt attention. I never take well-mannered teenagers for granted. I always comment on it and thank them for being quiet. That day the Lord showed me how to use their good behavior as a teaching tool. I said to the several hundred high school students: "I want you to go with me in your imagination to my former homeland, Czechoslovakia, which is now behind the Iron Curtain. The educational system of Communism is very much like the kind the Nazis used for me. If you were going to a Communist school you most likely would sit as quietly and well-behaved there as you do in this American school auditorium. Any difference? In a Communist or Nazi school you sit quietly because you know what happens if you don't. Any disturbance is punished swiftly, especially if the school could be embarrassed before an outsider. The principle would take hold of your neck and lead you to a detention cell where you could think it over for a few days with bread and water to sustain you. You'd think twice before you would take such a risk, wouldn't you?

"Now, why have you been sitting still in this rather hot auditorium for most of a class period? Are you afraid of your principal? I met him, he is a rather nice fellow." After the laughter had settled down among the listeners, I continued, "Your teachers wouldn't lock you up just because you got out of line, would they? So why are you decent, respectful, and well behaved? I'll tell you why. You *choose* to be! So nobody has to force you, threaten you, bribe you, manipulate you. You are the youth of a free nation. You are Americans! You have a freedom of choice and you are quiet because you want to be, not because you have to be."

Every time I use this little illustration, and by now I have done so hundreds of times, I still get the same lump in my throat when I look into the astonished open faces of every American audience I tell it to. Parents and teachers look as amazed as the youngsters do.

I shall never forget when one woman came up to me after a high school assembly. She had slipped in through a side door to listen, and she said to me, "Oh, Hansi, I am the mother of twelve children but I have never *once* taught them about freedom."

I fought back tears and said, "Go home and start at

once."

I say the same to teachers, youth leaders, and parents alike. "Don't lament your neglect of the past. We cannot change the indifference of lost years. But we can begin *now* to do something about the future. I do not guarantee that we adults will always win a popularity contest among our youth by teaching and demanding such old-fashioned values as self-control, a full hour's work for a full hour's pay, honesty, respect, and most of all, the willingness to accept the invisible ultimate authority of God as our standard of behavior."

I might get standing ovations when I speak to youth groups, but daily teaching in classrooms and at home is less glamorous. I have done both in my lifetime and I am still doing both.

Slowly, I watch my own children mature, one by one, as they begin to understand my teaching about working for a living, and that freedom is not free after all. It's hard to swim upstream, and I often feel that's what is demanded of me.

My children are all-American, and that their mother was a former Nazi, who fled from a Communist labor camp and once nearly starved to death does not make them different from the rest of the American youth. They never missed a meal and have lived in freedom all their lives and cannot help but take it as much for granted as anyone else with a "normal" parent. So they act the way their peers do. They have gotten resentful and angry at me because their friends played while they worked. They looked with justifiable envy at the parents who gave their children a nice car for high school graduation. It is not within the grasp of young people in any generation to look at those less fortunate than they are and count their own blessings. I don't know if my own children appreciate freedom any more than the average American does, but I have *one* hope: I tried to put the seed of understanding into their souls from childhood on. They know about Jesus and salvation. They know how freedom works. They can never say that they did not know the great works of the Lord which He did for us and our land. I am convinced they *will* remember, but how can thousands of American youth remember if nobody ever taught it to them?

Betty and I have dedicated our lives to go from place to place to teach, explain, and refresh America's memory before it is too late. We thank God for the privilege, but sometimes it is just hard work with exhausting demands. Right now we are both very tired.

New Year's Eve Again/
Thursday

Another wedding, another couple on their honeymoon. Last year it was Tim. This Christmas it's my Heidi. She married a fine young man who is in the Air Force and medical school at the same time. Money is tight for them but Heidi arranged a beautiful ceremony. She did all her own flower decorations and, between her friends and siblings, she planned a heartwarming occasion. After the wedding I spent several days with my children in Palm Springs. The newlyweds interrupted their honeymoon to be with us on Christmas Eve and we all had a warm, sunny, fun-time together.

It was a good ending to the past year. I wish I could say the whole year was as pleasant!

This last year has been full of learning for me, but rough, very rough. As I watch my children leave and return from their honeymoons, very happy and deeply in love, I recall that this last year I have wondered several times if my honeymoon with my Omnipotent Husband is over? Have I failed somewhere?

Maybe it began wrong because I felt so tired and completely burned out. December is usually my month to rest, write, catch up with the family and my friends. But by January I found myself so exhausted that I did not know how I could face the new year with a full schedule all confirmed and set to go.

I shall never forget the special conversation I had with the Lord one early morning at the beginning of this year. I was sitting on the carpet in our living room watching the rain pelt the window and gray clouds cover our usually sunny California sky. I felt depressed and grumpy. "Lord," I said aloud, "other people at our

age begin to plan for retirement and a rocking chair. I
look at our schedule and I get a sinking feeling in the pit
of my stomach. The whole year looks like a big mountain, too high to climb."

While I spoke, a Bible picture flashed before my inner
eye. Betty had taught it several times on our last tour
and I love her illustrations. She and I have something
in common: when we read, write, speak, or teach we
"see" everything in our imagination. Whenever she
reads chapter 14 in the book of Joshua, I see Joshua
standing before the people of Israel, dividing the land.
Up walks a very old man, erect, dignified, with a
flowing white beard and silvery long hair. He says:
"Thou knowest the thing that the Lord said unto
Moses...And now, behold, the Lord hath kept me alive...
and now, lo, I am this day fourscore and five years
old.... Now therefore give me this mountain" (vv.6,10,
12).

Oh, Caleb, how can you ask for one of the hardest jobs
at your advanced age of eighty-five years? Didn't you
know how impossible it was to conquer enemies who
had the advantage of the heights as your warriors
climbed toward them? Was not an army destined for
disaster in Bible times if they had to start an attack
below a mountain?

Yes, Caleb knew it. He had been a spy forty-five years
before. Now he asked for the place he had spied out.
"And Hebron therefore became the inheritance of
Caleb...because that he wholly followed the Lord God of
Israel" (v.14).

"Give me this mountain," I thought. "But do I want to
say it, Lord?"

"You don't have to," Jesus answered ever so gently.
"And I will not be angry with you. I'll give you your
cabin and your rocking chair that you dream about. I'll
understand."

"Would you be sad, Lord?" I wondered in my heart.

"Remember what happened because most of the
Israelites did what you long to do," Jesus reminded me.

And I thought of another Bible text that always tugs on my heartstrings when Betty quotes it: "And there remaineth yet very much land to be possessed" (Josh. 13:1). The Israelites never completed the possession of the land God had promised to them, and the Old Testament is full of the heartbreaking results. Because the parents got tired of struggle and conquest, they settled down and tried to coexist with evil. Their children accepted the way of idolatry and forgot that they would lose the land if they turned from the God of their fathers.

What an example of warning for America! Why is evil spreading like a cancer in our Christian nation? Because most of the "silent majority" does nothing to stop it. We just sit and complain about the moral decay we observe.

"Give me that mountain," I said aloud and Betty looked up from her book. She smiled and nodded.

"I knew you would want to go on and so do I," she said. "After all, we're not even eighty-five years old!"

"No, we are not," I grinned, "but sometimes I feel like it. Nevertheless, we better practice what we preach, teacher."

Little did I know what it meant. The first few meetings went well and I started to gather courage. After a weekend at an Air Force base on the West Coast Betty seemed to come down with a heavy cold or allergy attack. We weren't quite sure what the real problem was.

Sneezing and coughing, she placed herself behind the steering wheel of our motor home and we left for the Midwest. We were scheduled to pick up several appointments in some Southern states on our way. Shortly after we pulled away, I came down with a severe sore throat and I began to cough, too. This came as a surprise. I have various physical limitations, but I hardly ever catch a cold or any other bronchial problem.

Through all the years Betty and I had traveled and worked together, we had never been sick at the same time. One always could cover for the other if one of us became indisposed, which was seldom indeed.

We tried to hide from each other how ill we felt. And we *did* speak at all our appointments in the South. By the time we arrived in the Midwest, my throat had turned a deep red, Betty could hardly sit up to drive because her coughing had made her back and stomach muscles so sore. Every move caused her pain.

I shall never forget one miserable night in a small motel room in a rural community. I had to speak at a youth banquet for a Christian school. I dislike speaking for banquets because the program is invariably too long and it seems that the speaker is added as an after-thought. When all is eaten, said, and done and the audience is ready to go home, the speaker is finally introduced. If I had had my way I would have given the benediction and sent everybody home. Betty and I sat for three hours, trying to suppress our coughs. I finally gave a short message and we left for the motel. We couldn't hook up the motor home, so we parked it outside and stayed in the tiny, musty-smelling room.

Betty got increasingly worse, she wheezed, fought to get enough air, choked under coughing spells and finally whispered between her labored breathing, "Are you mad at me? You look angry."

I answered between coughs: "No, I am not mad at you. I am angry at God." Betty's face showed utter amazement. "Look, Betty," I said agitatedly, "we have been praying for weeks to be healed. The reason why we keep going is our commitment to God and the people. These communities have worked months to prepare for our meetings. It simply didn't seem fair to cancel at the last minute. We have gone from place to place believing that we would get better. We are getting worse, my dear. I know what some of our charismatic friends would say. 'If you only believe, you could be healed in an instant.' Betty, I have no problem believ-ing that He can heal us. I *know* He can do it. One move of His hand and we would be well. The reason I am

angry is that I know He *can* do it, but He is *not* doing it,
though we have asked Him over and over again."

Betty was too sick to answer and I was sorry I had
disturbed her more with my outbursts.

All I had available was a little electrical coffee pot. I
boiled water, dipped a washcloth into it and put the hot
moist cloth on her throat, covering it with a dry towel to
keep it warm. After a while I watched her relax enough
to fall into a fitful sleep.

I turned off the light, crawled into my bed and said,
"Jesus, are You still around? I am sorry I blew up, for
Your sake and for Betty's sake. It seems You have
forsaken us and I don't know why. We have searched
our hearts to see if any sin blocks the channel. We've
asked You to reveal to us if we have done something
displeasing to You. I have asked for help, directions,
and wisdom. Lord, if I call in a doctor we'll both be in
the hospital by morning, and we still have three
meetings to cover this weekend. Please, show me what
to do."

I felt so hot and sick and Jesus seemed to be so very
far away, but I thought I heard Him say, "You may go to
the hospital or you can trust Me. I will see you through."

"I thought I trusted You for these long weeks already,
Jesus," I said softly while the tears began to roll. "I
believe that You are my Husband. Would a loving
husband let his wife suffer like this if it was in his power
to heal her? We both know that You could heal us in an
instant."

"Let's talk about it when you feel better," the Lord
seemed to say.

I cried myself to sleep. The following morning I felt a
bit revived. Through all those painful days I had been
deeply thankful that neither of us had lost our voices
completely. Our only problem was that our bad coughs
would tickle our voice boxes to the point that we could
not speak until the coughing spasm subsided.

We watched each other closely. When we saw the
other go into such a spell, we would just walk to the

microphone and take over for the other. Most of the time the audiences didn't even know we had a problem. They thought we had planned a combined lecture. Nobody knew how sick we were and nobody believed that we were seriously ill. When I called our office and spoke with our office manager, who has left since then, I asked for special prayer. She assured me that everybody was fighting the flu and to stop worrying, we would soon be over it.

I suggested to Betty that she should remain in the motel and I would cover her Sunday School lesson.

"If you can go, I can, too," she said. And the three of us — the Lord, Betty, and I — marched ourselves to the church.

During Sunday School she did fine, and I made it through the church service also. They had a church potluck dinner and Betty was asked to tell some Bible stories for the young people. Her way of storytelling takes lots of breath and toward the end I watched her struggle. Her throat was closing. I walked up. She finished her sentence and handed me the mike. She walked off and I finished the message. The audience clapped and cheered, they thought we had planned it all for a special effect. People began to beg for one more story. Somebody who had heard Betty before asked for the story of the little boy who gave his lunch to Jesus. No doubt that story is one of Betty's trademarks.

Betty and I looked at each other. It takes unusual breath control to tell it right and it has no breaking point. We both knew I could not take over. I watched my partner take a deep breath and walk back to the speaker's podium.

I always pray when she speaks, she does the same when I speak, but I never prayed harder. I held my breath in her stead. I spent so much energy I felt weak when she had finished and the people went wild with clapping and enthusiasm. These precious listeners will never know what struggles and victories took place behind our smiling, outwardly composed faces.

I got the same test in the evening. I had to give my message in a community meeting on the healing of America. Betty and I knew that it was one of the topics that she could not come up to the microphone to rescue me. I stepped behind the pulpit, fighting physical dizziness and an upset stomach, besides the cough. Worse than my physical condition was my inner confusion. My emotions felt raw, my mental outlook foggy and groping. Did I have anything to say?

"Jesus," I pleaded desperately, "You seem so far away. I lost my sense of closeness to You and I feel afraid. If You have nothing to say we can quit before I ever open my mouth. Please, speak through me."

I had no idea if I was communicating to the audience or not, I was too preoccupied with holding on to the pulpit and to Jesus while I spoke. When I watched the people rise for a standing ovation at the end, my tears began to roll.

"This was one of the best messages you ever gave," Betty whispered when I returned to my seat beside her.

"Thank You, Jesus," I whispered and had to walk out because I felt a coughing spell coming on. I had not coughed once during the whole program.

We did not have any engagements until the following weekend and then only one Sunday afternoon meeting in a small church way out in the country. After stocking up with needed groceries, we found a quiet camping place and hooked up the motor home right beside a murmuring brook. There were no other campers at the campground. The stillness was only interrupted by singing birds, humming bumblebees, and some far-away barking dogs.

Warmth and sunshine surrounded us every day and we walked in the nearby woods. My favorite spring green sprouted everywhere, with a deep-blue sky overhead and flowers nodding in the gentle wind. I began to feel better.

"Lord," I prayed, "I thought You said that we would talk about our problems after I felt better. Can we talk about them now?"

"Why don't you read the book of Job together while you are resting up," the Lord seemed to suggest.

I conveyed the message to Betty. I didn't know if it was really the Lord's direction, I wasn't sure of anything anymore. Neither was she, but we decided that it had to be His idea because we wouldn't have thought of it. We took turns reading to each other aloud. Whenever a cough stopped us the other would take over. Then we would think about what we read and discuss it. It was mind-boggling. Both of us thought we knew the book. We had read it several times before in younger years when we had tried to read through the whole Bible.

What insights we got this time. What emotions, what strengths, and what final victories! "If He slays me, yet will I trust in Him," Job cried out. He was covered with painful boils. His children had all been killed and his foolish wife insulted him, his friends accused him, and his apparently revengeful God punished him for sins he couldn't recall.

"Lord," I said aloud after reading that chapter to Betty, "is that what You are trying to teach us in a more gentle way? Are Job's words in that text the highest form of trust a human being can reach for?"

"No," the Lord answered, "there is one more step. The highest form of trust a human being can learn is when there is no more 'if.'"

Betty and I talked about it. We didn't understand the Lord's words. We knew it was His teaching, we couldn't have come up with such a strange conclusion. What could be harder to attain than the decision to stay faithful to Him even *if* God apparently turned angry and unreasonable? We both prayed and meditated much as we puzzled over such mysteries.

"Lord, please explain it to us," I pleaded over and over. "We are both Your dumb kids, You know."

"Why don't you read on," Jesus encouraged me. "You will find the answer in the same book."

We both knew what the Lord meant when we read

Job's final words of victory six chapters later: "For *I know* that my Redeemer liveth,.....yet in my flesh I shall see God" (Job 19:25-26, italics added).

Betty and I looked at each other in wordless surprise, tears in our eyes. Of course, this was the ultimate trust. No more "if," only a triumphant "I know" in spite of all the agonies. Nothing had changed for Job at that point. He was as sick, bereaved, confused, and accused as before, but his spirit had conquered his dying body.

I laid my head down on that familiar text and let my tears roll. It was one of those moments when the Lord washed my eyes with tears so that my soul could see again. I cried part of my confusion away and I asked the Lord to forgive me.

"I do not know where I stand in my spiritual maturity," I said to my divine Husband. "I don't even know if I have reached the 'if' stage yet. But, Lord, I do want to learn to trust You completely, without the 'if.' I want to know that I know. I ask You to teach me, Jesus, and I ask for the willingness to be willing. I want it though I am a bit afraid of it. It seems such a terribly hard thing to learn."

Betty prayed a similar prayer. I know because she told me so.

The Lord encouraged us to finish reading the book of Job before we left for the next appointment. We rejoiced with Job when the Lord "turned the captivity of Job when he prayed for his friends."

I realized again that there can be no healing and a turning of events unless there is first forgiveness. Job had to forgive and pray for those who had harassed him thinking they were doing God a favor. Then the Lord drew my attention to a text I had never seen before: "Then came there unto him all his brethren, and all his sisters, and all they that had been of his acquaintance before...and comforted him; every man gave him a piece of money, and... a ring of gold" (42:11).

I had renewed peace and felt physically stronger when we left our secluded camping spot for the next meeting.

I shall never forget the tiny country church I spoke in that Sunday afternoon. They took a love offering and brought the money to us before we left. It was not a giant sum and I didn't expect any big gifts. The audience was too poor for that. But someone had put a small gold ring into the offering plate, a ring with a yellow stone. It appeared to be the size that would fit on the small hand of a teenager or a young woman.

The giver will never know what she did for me. I hope I can thank her in eternity. Jesus has no other hands or feet on this earth but those of His children. Someone listened and obeyed so that my Husband could send me a physical message when I needed it above the inner still small voice He usually assures me with. I have received other gifts before and after but I shall forever treasure that gift of love. I wonder if Job felt as overwhelmed as I did when he received his first ring of comfort from his friends. Bless the giver, dear Lord.

* * * * * * * *

Betty and I were not instantly healed. My cough hung on for months. Betty is still bothered with bronchial problems. Up to this day we have never missed a meeting, and God willing, we don't intend to. We finished the spring tour as scheduled and also a long hard fall tour. Our yearly Israel-Europe tour went well and the Lord had a surprise for me before our annual "Hansi" retreat on the West Coast.

"I want you to teach the book of Job," the Lord informed me when I asked Him for the topics that would be recorded on master tapes.

I was more than surprised, I felt scared. I have never felt competent or worthy to teach the Bible. A Bible scholar like Betty can do that, but a former Nazi who never attended a Bible seminary in her life should not attempt such a great undertaking — unless the Lord says so.

He said it and I did it, with shaky knees, literally. I don't know how much it helped the listeners but it became a tremendous blessing for me, and Job is fast becoming one of my favorite Bible characters.

I want to learn to trust like Job, but it makes me afraid. This is a strange contradiction and Betty and I have talked about it several times. Since those jarring weeks of last spring we both have had a running battle with fear. We don't accept it and try not to give in to it. We know better! It is another aspect of God's teaching for us, I am sure, but I am slow to learn no matter how eagerly I try.

I would have a hard time describing the problem. The honeymoon with my Lord consisted of a joyful assurance that I was under His complete protection. No matter what happened, I felt that Betty and I were sitting under a bulletproof glass cover, so to speak, and the devil could not get to us. Even when I nearly died of food poisoning, the sense of God's presence never left either one of us. But suddenly something changed and I don't know why. Someone removed the cover and I don't know who did it.

Betty and I both feel vulnerable and unsure. The confidence that Jesus will always keep any evil away from us is no longer in our immediate reach. We struggle for it, fight constant fear that another disaster is around the corner, that God will demand more show of blind obedience from us.

I shall never forget Betty's troubled face before we left for this year's fall tour. Among the many problems that beset our spring tour was the unreliable performance of our old motor home. We barely got it home to park it in our usual storage yard. A week before we had to leave this fall, we had not received word from the Lord what to do about the ailing vehicle. We had not taken it in for a tuneup either. We simply didn't know how to proceed.

"Do you think the Lord wants to test our faith more by taking the motor home on the road without a tuneup?" Betty said and her lips trembled though she tried to keep a steady voice.

My heart went out to her. She seldom loses her

composure and I realized the deep struggle in her soul.

"I have told the Lord that I am willing to do it if that is what I should do," she continued. "He is driving anyway, but He has to provide me with the strength to handle the unpredictable thing."

I interrupted her: "No Betty, I cannot believe that this is required of you. A husband might test his wife but he would never ask her to do an irrational thing. To go out on the road without a good checkup would not be a test of faith but foolishness and presumption. But I am glad that you told the Lord you were willing to do it." I wondered in my heart if it was still all right with Jesus if I spoke so confidently of His care and love, but I had to.

If things had changed so drastically that my former convictions were no longer valid, we didn't need to leave for another tour anyway! Both of us would no longer have the authority to convince people. All we could talk about would be the fear of the Lord, and I had no burden to do that. Too many messages are already given to scare people into heaven. I thought we had passed that point years ago and fallen in love with Him. There is no fear in love. I had taught it countless times to many audiences and individuals. Would I have to eat my own words?

No, I did not have to do that! We rolled out in a brand new motor home one week later. We had a good tour, and I shall never forget one afternoon when we drove up a country road in Pennsylvania through several periods of thunderstorms. It had rained off and on, and before us towered the darkest masses of clouds we had ever seen. We seemed to drive right into them. When the cloudburst hit, the road disappeared before our eyes. We didn't have to concern ourselves with traffic. Out of the corners of our eyes we could see cars parked all along the side of the road as we drove past them.

Both of us watched the ditches on each side of the road as our guide to stay on the pavement. Even small passenger cars dared not drive but had pulled over. Our high vehicle swayed in the vicious winds. The windshield had a leak and I sent a fast question up to the Lord: "Do you want us to stop, Jesus?"

"No, you don't have to," the Lord came through loud and clear. "But if Betty wants to stop, she may."

"Do you want to pull over?" I called to Betty over the noise of the storm.

"Did the Lord say we should?" she called back.

"No," I hollered without taking my eyes off the road. "He said that you could if you wanted to."

"We'll drive on until He tells us to stop," Betty said, and I was not surprised. We both had to overcome another bout with fear, but we knew we would never permit the old devil to tell us what to do. We would drive until the Lord told us to stop.

The rain quit as if someone had removed a heavy curtain within a single moment. We drove from blinding rain into bright sunshine and a deep blue sky. It startled us both as we sat back and relaxed. I had never seen such a sudden change from storm to a cloudless sky in my whole life. Neither had Betty. We talked about it. The Lord gave Betty a sentence we shall never forget.

"Those who are afraid are still in the storm," Jesus said to the little brave woman at the steering wheel. She repeated His words to me and we sat in astonished silence for many miles of driving in bright sunshine. What a statement, what a truth! I am not sure I understand it all completely even now. I think it means that sometimes we have to simply struggle through instead of waiting it out until the danger is past.

The last year has been a struggle on every side. Shall I call it a marriage crisis? If so, I am fully aware that it was mine, not the Lord's. I want to believe that the Lord's message to Betty proved that we are learning our lessons. We can start the new year hopefully, with less stormy weather and with a new beginning.

There is new staff in the office: the best we ever had. We are driving a new motor home. We have a new outlook on life.

"Oh, Lord, grant us a blessed new year and give me back my honeymoon joy. I lost it when I had my first big quarrel with You and I long to get it back. Teach me to trust You completely!" This is my heartfelt prayer for the new year!

Another New Year's Eve/
Friday

It has almost become a tradition for me to come back to this diary at the end of every year for retrospection and evaluation. Reading my last sentence of the previous entry, I can only smile and repeat what I have said so often in my lectures: "Don't pray for anything unless you really mean it. God will take you up on your requests and do what you asked for."

Through the years Betty and I have prayed; "Teach us to trust You, dear Lord, completely."

He is teaching us and at times I would prefer easier lessons or a break. I had confident hope that this past year would be less burdensome than the previous one, but it was not to be. The nature of our problems changed a bit. Our health did not give out as drastically as last year. My oldest daughter suggested, after it was all over, that we both might have suffered with a walking pneumonia as her mother-in-law did. She ended up in the hospital under an oxygen tent during the fateful flu season of last year.

We had no flu attack this past year, but Betty's allergies haven't settled down since her illness. My stomach is always unpredictable since I have only one-third left. Any crisis usually results in an upset tummy for me. But this past year I had a constant battle with headaches besides. To know that it runs in my family doesn't take the pain away.

Betty gets tired of her stuffy nose and cough. I get weary of hurting all the time. But as long as we are able to function, we try to ignore our aging bodies and do not consider it an insurmountable obstacle.

Our big problem this year was low finances. I know
we are not the only organization that has financial
difficulties at this time. The whole nation has been
going through a deep recession and our support rises
and falls with the American economy. We are interde-
nominational and not backed by any particular church
or charity. We serve the grass-root Christians of many
denominations and are supported by individual dona-
tions and freewill offerings collected at our meetings.
The sales of our books and tapes after the meetings and
by mail order have been crucial for our minimum
subsistence for longer than just this trying year.

To be honest, this last year wasn't that much more
difficult than the years before. The ministry has existed
for seven years now. We began in reverse order, we had
our seven lean years first. We never had any fat years to
lay up storage as it happened in one of my favorite Bible
stories.

I started out with my retirement fund after I had
resigned as a teacher. From the beginning, my staff
and I had nothing else to count on but the promises of
God. It was enough! We never had surplus, but we were
always able to pay the bills and expand, one little step
at a time. Sometimes payroll would be a bit late, but the
Lord and God's people always came through.

And if the truth is told, it worked itself out again this
past year. Looking back, I have to admit that the bills
remained current, we had no savings or debts, payroll
was up to date, and the Lord kept us afloat. Looking
around I have seen several organizations dissolve in
bankruptcy; churches are in the red or deep in debt and
every day I get stacks of letters pleading for money.
Some of the senders are fine servants of God and
friends of mine.

Why then was the last year so extremely hard on me
and my trust in the Lord?

I know that our financial struggle got to me because I
did not anticipate it. I thought we were over the worst

when we cancelled our weekly TV program, our daily radio broadcast and stripped expenditures to the bone. I had complete confidence that our new staff and Betty and I could ride out the economic storm because we were so united and committed to serve God and America with all our hearts. We still are, and I shall thank God forever that He brought us the best co-workers for this crisis year. We prayed together and we worked together and they all stood behind me in my personal struggle with much silent prayer. I am just now finding out *how* supportive everybody was.

I believe that Satan increases his dirty attacks when we are tired. He knows our weak spots and a weary Christian forgets to put on the whole armor of God.

I still wonder what brought on my excessive tiredness. Did it begin in my soul or body? I have always believed that I can conquer the world if I have peace of mind. I don't know what went first. Did I overwork? I know my tendency to be a workaholic, but I try to stay on top of it, forcing myself to get enough sleep and exercise.

When did I lose my peace of mind? When the Lord didn't act the way I predicted? Must I eat every word I teach?

Betty and I have said it often enough: true love is when we trust God even though we cannot understand His dealing with us. It's easy to trust Him when we write the script and He blesses it dutifully.

Well, Jesus chose not to follow my script this last year at all. Satan came at us from every side, it seemed. And the more we prayed and worked together, the harder it got. Payroll became a nightmare to me. February is always a trying month but we had some of God's greatest miracles in years past during that time of year. However, there was no miracle this February. Instead we had our first audit by the IRS.

I was not afraid of its outcome. We had nothing to hide and every penny was accounted for, but our vulnerability lay in the bookkeeping of the past.

Because of our small beginnings we had never been able to hire well-trained, experienced administration personnel. We had several younger women who did their best and helped out because they wanted to serve the Lord, but I was deeply aware of our incomplete and sometimes antiquated office procedures.

The new staff is highly competent. The office manager and part-time treasurer had been with us less than a year and were in the midst of updating and refiling when the IRS agent made his appearance.

My heart sank when I saw him. He spoke only broken English, had come from Egypt a few years ago and we were "training ground" for him. Betty and I knew what to expect. For a man with a middle eastern background one thing is paramount. He has to keep face. He *had* to find some discrepancy in order to prove himself to his boss.

Our new treasurer is a retired widow who has one shortcoming. She is kind and accommodating to a fault. And she outdid herself to meet the gentleman's demands. She spent whole weekends reconstructing inadequate records, going through hundreds of receipts. Thank God we had saved them all.

By the third week of the audit, I had to stay out of the office. My anger and frustration had built to the point where I wasn't sure if I could stay friendly and polite around the gentleman any longer.

When the man "inspected" our warehouse he discovered some of my former household goods stored in the back. Among the stuff was a lawn mower. I had given it to the ministry so that either a staff member could use it or we could someday sell it and put the money where it was most needed. Our treasurer did not know the details and since I wasn't around to be asked she said it was Betty's and my lawn mower.

"Get it out of here," the man informed her. "You have no right to store any private property in a non-profit warehouse."

I did not know that I still could get as angry as I did

when I was told about it over the phone. I couldn't sleep or eat and I am afraid Betty got most of my explosion. "I never thought I would watch Gestapo tactics in America," I fumed. "Who does the man think he is? How can such a thing happen in a free country?"

The lawn mower was immediately sold, of course, and I told my office staff that they would have to see the audit through to the end. I would do my part and stay away, otherwise they would have more on their hands than our faulty bookkeeping of past years.

Their patience, endurance, and Christian graciousness prevailed, and the agent finished his work after three weeks, and was satisfied.

A few weeks later we received a letter that gave us complete clearance with one correction: our CPA had made a recording error on one of the tax forms. We were warned not to do it again. The accountant had long since retired and it was not even a bookkeeping mistake made in our own office.

"You mean we passed with flying colors?" I asked our very tired but jubilant treasurer.

"Did you expect anything less?" she smiled. "Wouldn't God honor your faithful ministry?"

It took weeks before my stomach settled down and my knotty nerves untied so I could finally sit down and figure out why the whole deal got me so agitated. The IRS man most likely didn't do anything wrong and tried to do his job. Why do I still feel angry every time I remember those stressful weeks, even now? I believe I have become more an American than the Americans born in this land.

If this had happened in Nazi Germany, I would have perceived this particular agent as pleasant. No doubt, a Gestapo man would have been meaner and his questions would have been less polite.

I am so sensitive to the issue of freedom that I overreact. I am aware of it and the staff knows it too. The Lord, of course, tries to teach me to swing to a sensible middle. And the devil knows how to aggravate me with the extreme. I get frustrated every time I see anybody's personal freedom, or any other freedom, threatened.

* * * * * * * *

We left for the spring tour with the recent happenings still fresh on our minds, knowing that payroll would be due and there weren't enough funds to pay our faithful workers or ourselves. None of us can boast reserves, we pay our bills out of every current pay check.

I felt raw inside. The Lord and I had never lost communication. I just didn't understand His messages to me. Betty had difficulties, too. Whenever I would storm into His presence about our financial plight, He would assure both of us repeatedly, "Money is not our problem."

Betty said it out loud one morning as we rolled along the Interstate highway: "Yes, Lord, money might not be Your problem but it certainly is ours at the present time. We simply don't know what You mean."

The Lord didn't explain His message but repeated it so often that after awhile Betty and I would say it to each other: "Money is *not* our problem."

I pondered over it for hours. "Lord, what *is* the problem? Please show us," I would plead.

"I will show you," the Lord would assure me. We were not on silent terms with each other and I talked more than ever, maybe too much. I did not listen enough. I was afraid that Jesus would answer me with more riddles. I already felt like a bird beating its head against a window—and my headaches increased.

Our first appointment was a women's retreat in an industrial midwestern state where the unemployment rate was sky high. The church camp is way out near a lake in a rural setting and very primitive. We drove past farmland and woods, even on gravel roads, to get there. The women who attended were from nearby farms and villages and certainly did not represent the wealthy class of America. I had not anticipated financial rewards and I knew when we accepted the invitation that we were responding for love's sake.

That was one reason I worried so much. Most of our appointments on the tour were of such nature and I was not even sure we could break even with travel expenses.

We arrived in the rain, and gray mist hovered over the lake. The leaders of the group acted shy and looked at us with uneasiness. The "staff cabin" was a simple place with bunk beds in small quarters, and all of us shared one bathroom and a tiny closet shower. Betty and I made some funny remarks and after the ice was broken, the pleasingly plump farmer's wife who was in charge confessed her worries. Would such primitive accommodations bother us?

Betty and I grinned and assured her that we had no complaints unless they had not brought any food. And they had plenty of that! The evening meal found everybody pleased and excited. The first meeting went well. I listened to the rain in the night and asked the Lord if it was His will to stop it for the sake of the many women who needed a time to visit and relax outdoors. The meeting place was too confining for social gatherings.

When I woke up to bright sunshine I was surprised. Somehow I had come to the place within the last few months I always expected just the opposite of my prayers. Jesus' wisdom knows best, I never have yet doubted His sovereignty. But I had lost my own confidence to the point where I didn't dare to ask freely anymore. I could never shake my fear that I was in for another disappointment, another battle with doubt and depression.

Two habits I clung to, though. First, every morning I would wake up and say, "I love You, Jesus." Next I would ask Him to teach me to trust Him completely for this day.

This particular morning, as I went for a walk, I thanked Him for the sunshine and the beauty of spring. My two favorite colors surrounded me: tender spring

green and deep blue sky. I asked Him to bring new life to
my soul, too. For more than a year now I had felt
alternately raw or numb and petrified inside.

I told the Lord I was willing to face financial or any
other problems as long as my inner harmony with Him
could be restored. I had a good cry and I suddenly
understood the words of the psalmist: "As the hart
panteth after the water brooks, so panteth my soul after
Thee, O God" (Psalm 42:1).

When the bell rang for breakfast I walked back along
the grassy path to the dining room. A younger lady
whom I had never seen before approached me and
handed me a slip of paper with a Scripture reference.
"The Lord wants you to read this text," she said. "I
don't understand it at all but He said you would know
what it is all about."

As soon as I could get to a Bible, I read the verses:
"For, lo, the winter is past, the rain is over and gone; the
flowers appear on the earth; the time of the singing of
birds is come, and the voice of the turtle is heard in our
land" (Song of Solomon 2:11-12).

The ice began to break in my soul that weekend. Betty
and I became good friends with many of the women, but
foremost with the members of the committee and the
president who had initiated these area retreats just
recently.

The beautiful weekend gave me such a lift, I didn't
even give it a thought whether they would take up an
offering. Maybe the people couldn't afford it.

Well, they did call for an offering. "Let each lady give
in proportion to what she has received and it was worth
to her," the president said. "Give as unto the Lord, and
ask Him to show you how much."

I shall never forget the beaming faces of the committee when they handed us the check. "We have *never*
had so much to give to any speaker before," Leta said.

I sat down and had a good cry again. I also did
something I very seldom do. I told them about our
financial emergency and how we certainly never

dreamed that God would provide through a group like theirs. "Between the offering and our splendid sales of books and tapes, we might be able to cover the payroll," I smiled through my tears. We all rejoiced together and parted as though we had known each other always. I am still in contact with the president. I consider her a personal friend and like a sister.

Praise the Lord! Most of the tour went unexpectedly well and money came from the least likely places. We not only broke even, we caught up with lagging payroll on top of the other bills which had to be paid on time.

Payroll is a tremendous monthly load on my heart. My paycheck is not my first concern, though I have to have money to pay many bills. It bothers me that my staff has to live with so much uncertainty. Betty resigned from a secure job and gave up retirement. Our office manager resigned from civil service and had to borrow money to pay off her pension fund when she came to work with us. Her friend, who is retired, had looked forward to free time but now she puts in countless unpaid hours to reorganize our bookkeeping.

Every time I talk to the Lord about it He reminds me kindly that the people are not working for me but for Him. "It's My ministry, is it not?" the Lord questions and I hasten to assure Him that it surely is His work.

Even before we returned to California another major crisis began to loom before us. Well, the short repose had obviously been too good to be true.

Our annual trip to Israel began to fall apart and the travel agent in the south who handled it seemed to encourage the problem. Another puzzle! "Lord," I cried out, "what is happening?"

"Trust Me, I shall see you through," was the only answer we got.

The upsets, perplexities, and half-hearted promises from our travel agent are too numerous to mention. Things got so bad that I went to the Lord and said, "I need clear orders. Shall we cancel the whole deal or is it still Your tour and Your will that we go?"

Betty and I got the same answer, unmistakably clear: "This is My tour," the Lord said, "I want you to go."

We flew with our hearts in our throats to New York. We had not even received the group tickets for the overseas portion yet and wondered if we would become one more stranded group at an airport. The travel agent did not have the time or courage to meet us personally but an office girl from the agency waited for us at the overseas ticket counter. She had the tickets. They had been issued by another travel agency. It deepened our misgivings. Would we end up stranded overseas? The agency was obviously tottering on the brink of financial disaster, though we had been assured otherwise. The young woman mumbled something that the crisis of the war in Lebanon had encouraged so many cancellations and she handed me a note to sign. We never make a profit on our overseas tours but this time I would owe the travel agency nearly three thousand dollars because we led the smallest group we ever had and that raised prices. I had no choice but to sign, and eighteen women boarded the plane to Israel. We had never had only women before, either, always some couples or even single men. This tour consisted of eighteen women who dared to go to Israel at the height of the Israeli war in Lebanon.

It was the best tour ever, and the Lord used us to encourage many Israeli people.

Our guide, David, waited at the airport. "I am sorry we are so few," I said to him, "but everybody seems to be scared of the PLO!"

He counted and his eyes lit up when he said, "The number eighteen stands for 'life' in Hebrew, it is a good number." His broad smile and attentive friendliness never revealed the fact that he had postponed a trip to the United States for us. He treated us as if we were the only group in Israel.

And it almost seemed that way. The hotels were nearly empty, the Israeli people downhearted. That eighteen American women dared to come when so many tours had cancelled cheered many hearts. We received royal treatment and got to see more than usual because we didn't need to wait anywhere. Israel was quiet and safer than ever before. The PLO was rather busy in Beirut. Border shellings were not a problem as they had been in years before, and David took us anywhere we wanted to go.

The group was amazed about many things, above all, about the way the American media handled the Lebanon conflict. American reporters obviously took the side of the PLO and didn't even give Israel a chance to tell their side of the story. Some of our women would call home and find their families in great fear for our lives while we enjoyed peace, tranquility and days of harmony.

The American media can agitate me to no end, and I better not get into the subject. They prove to me that freedom can be misused. A handful of liberal men can brainwash a whole nation by telling only one side of the story, and that is exactly what happened right before our eyes. I prayed a lot for a calm spirit; I can get so furious about lopsided news.

Well, our little group grew together, like one big family and, by the time we toured Europe, I thanked the Lord that He did not let me cancel. I also thanked Him for loyal friends. Our American travel agency had not paid tour expenses in advance, as is the custom, neither in Israel nor in Switzerland. But in both countries our guides are such friends that they had their own agencies cover for us, or we would have been stranded.

We saw God's hand everywhere and His love in sad eyes when we parted. I hate to say goodbye any time but it is hardest after our yearly tours. We always become like a family. Betty and I are painfully aware that, most likely, we will not see many of these new-found friends again until eternity.

This time it was harder yet because the tour group flew home to America without us.

* * * * * * *

Talking about tests of faith! The Lord had repeatedly informed me through the early months of the year that Betty and I would have to visit several Christian publishers in Europe. My book had been translated into German, Swedish, and Norwegian, among other languages, and the Lord wanted me to introduce our Bible study material to the foreign publishers who had translated my Hansi book.

At first I did not even give it my consideration. The whole idea sounded absurd and certainly not from the Lord. How could we afford the added expense? Neither the ministry nor our personal account had any extra money to spare. How could I burden our brave little treasurer with more bills?

I finally told Betty about the persistent nagging in my heart and asked her to find out where it came from. Most likely the old devil was torturing me with an impossible request. Was it one of those "angel of light" deceptions to wear me down?

"If it is," Betty said, "just say yes to it. Remember how often we teach that not until we are willing to go to China can we find out if God wants us to go?"

I grinned. Betty's China story is a favorite across the nation among Christians. We get much mail on it. Betty's first great struggle to make Jesus the Lord of her life took place during her teenage years. She was so afraid that the Lord wanted her to go to China that she fought His Lordship for years. When she finally agreed to do whatever He asked, Jesus informed her tenderly that she did not have to go to China to work for Him.

This has been the year where we have to put into practice what we teach. "If it is Your will that we visit the publishers, we shall go," I prayed, hoping that Jesus would assure me otherwise.

But it was not another China story. We both got word to make preparations for it. I wrote letters to the publishers. I inquired about travel arrangements. We decided on a fifteen-day Eurailpass which permitted us to use any train, anywhere on the European continent and we could travel first class. We figured, if we traveled at night, we could sleep on the train and save hotel bills.

With great reluctance, I told the office staff about the extra costs. We couldn't pay it all ourselves. Their response was heartwarming. "Don't worry about it. If the Lord wants you both to go, He will provide for it."

I did worry about it. Somehow I did not seem to be able to shake the financial pressures for most of this long, rough year. I also ended up apologizing to the Lord continually for my doubts because He *did* see us through.

We scraped from bill to bill, from month to month, and sometimes we suffered needlessly, like when we visited the publishers in Europe.

We didn't eat right and traveled too long on trains because I was so worried we would run out of money. However, we came back with extra traveler's checks and complete physical exhaustion. Europe had a heat wave in July and we could find little relief. Trains and cheap hotels have no air conditioners, neither do private homes of friends we stayed with. Normally Europe is cool for our California blood, but this time we not only returned prostrate from the heat but emotionally drained. The publishers received us kindly and promised to look at our material. But the moral decay and churchlessness of the European countries put a new burden on our souls.

In Communist countries people are not allowed to worship in Christian churches. In Europe's free world people don't feel the need to attend church and are proud of it. "Good Christians go three times in their lives to church," a Norwegian guide joked good-naturedly when I asked her about church life in her land, "when we are born, when we are confirmed and when we die. Fanatics go once every year to church, on Christmas Eve."

I had a hard time smiling about it. Young people of the various countries were willing to talk to us freely.

Almost everyone spoke English. They do not see any
need for marriage unless they want children. Dress
codes in public places do not exist, sex in public is
permissible, so is drug use. We watched policemen
turning their backs while young men injected themselves. In Stockholm we interrupted our stroll to ask for
interpretation of some Swedish banners at a big
demonstration. The people, mostly young, were demon-
strating *for* the Ayatollah Khomeini of Iran.

I shall never be the same again whenever I remember
Europe. We are praying for a revival. It is needed and
Europeans don't even realize it anymore. We here in
America once received our spiritual heritage from
European shores. Our best repayment could be our
consistent prayer for new spiritual life in these nations.

People have asked me where I see a difference
between America and Germany, for instance. All of
Germany was once the land of the Reformation — so
was Sweden and Norway where the Lutheran faith is a
state religion and the preachers are paid by the government. In America I am watching religious fires burn
low in our spiritual apathy. We Christians must unite
ourselves in a new prayer revival and pray that the
Holy Spirit will blow into our dying embers and revive
us to a new awakening. It has happened before. In
Europe I found cold ashes. I couldn't even detect a few
sparks on a national level. The Reformation has burned
itself out and higher and lower criticism has destroyed
the power of the simple gospel. The people are proud of
their intellectual approach. The churches are empty
and humanism has embraced existentialism for an
intoxicating new philosophy. The youngsters are full of
it, and of other inebriating drinks. Alcoholism is ram-
pant all over Europe, but the northern countries got to
me. We saw groups of young people everywhere, drink-
ing and rallying, and with no place to go to find valid
answers for their searching questions.

What an opening for the deceptive teaching of Marx-
ism! My soul shudders when I think that America

could go in the same direction.

We returned home with new determination to work for America's needed prayer revival.

We also had no time to overcome our jet lag, we had to prepare immediately for our fall tour, a long and busy schedule of ten weeks.

While my soul troubled itself about Europe's problems, another test sneaked up on us almost overnight as we washed, selected and packed our clothing for fall.

We had hand-carried our good clothing all over Europe so we would not lose it. Normally, we do not take our best speaker's outfits overseas. This time we had to meet with the publishers, so I had taken some of my favorite suits along. I thought I had the Lord's assurance that He would watch over our stuff. Not until we landed in New York did I put the carry-on bag on the baggage cart to be checked through, after customs had cleared us.

The airline lost our clothing bag on the final stretch home and I felt bewildered. "We normally trace luggage within thirty-six hours," the friendly agent assured us. We filled out papers. Since the office staff was on vacation I gave him our unlisted home number. After thirty-six hours, we called. They had no trace of the missing pieces. I went to the Lord.

"I thought You promised me Your watch-care over our luggage when I asked You if I dared to pack my best stuff," I said. "It's not the clothing itself, dear Lord — as much as I hate to lose it; it's my obvious inability to understand You right. When You said that You would take care of it, I thought You would hold on to it for us."

I do not think that any other problem has gotten more under our skin this year than that lost clothing bag. Maybe I should say it was the Lord's answer that got us so flustered.

"Did I say it was lost?" the Lord said to both of us.

"No, the airline says so," I cried, I was so mystified. "They assure us that it is stolen."

"It is neither stolen nor lost," the Lord repeated

Himself over and over as the days went by.

We had one more day before we had to roll out with our motor home. And the airline made things more difficult because we couldn't even sign insurance forms to cover the theft until the tenth day. We would be gone by then.

As we walked into our deserted office to load the books and tapes, the Lord spoke to Betty: "Turn on the answering service."

She did and almost unintelligibly because of a weak battery, we were able to get the needed key words. The name of another airline, our luggage at their lost-and-found station, and "your machine needs attention."

Betty made the needed phone calls and our bag was delivered to our door at midnight.

I have seldom cried harder with sheer relief. After the bag was back, not one piece of clothing disturbed, I confessed to Betty my great dilemma: "I felt I could not go on another tour and speak with assurance when I knew in my heart I had lost my sweet communion with the Lord. He had suddenly become inapproachable. I was afraid to drive out on the road if I couldn't be sure about my understanding of His directions anymore." Betty agreed with me. She had battled the same fears.

* * * * * * * *

We left with renewed confidence and the Lord gave us a successful and good tour. Moneywise we were able to send enough to the office to not only cover expenses but pay off some summer bills that had accumulated. Things were not going badly, so I could not understand why I felt as if I had come to the end. We were rolling westward after the tour and had to go right into the annual Hansi retreat after we got home.

Maybe I felt ill-prepared for the new messages we would record on master tapes. Maybe I felt just completely exhausted. The trip was hot and tiring. The motor home overheated and acted up. "Lord," I said, while the glaring highway stretched like a quivering endless white band before us in the desolate desert plains of New Mexico, "I thought I tried to trust You the best I know how."

"That is true," the Lord said.

"Trusting You takes so much energy," I said to Him, "and I have no more energy left. I feel completely drained. What if I cannot go on any longer?"

"You may quit," the Lord answered gently.

"You will not be angry at me if I quit the mountain climbing?" I asked.

"No, I will not be angry," the Lord assured me.

"I think I want to quit, Lord," I mulled over those words for a time. "I mean it this time."

"You may do so," the Lord answered.

I sat and felt a great relief flood my tense body. Knowing that I would meet with the entire board at our retreat I tried to formulate an explanation to them and a final thank-you speech to everyone. I fell asleep in the middle of my ponderings while Betty drove and prayed. She told me later that she sensed that I was in the middle of an immense struggle. When I woke up, I continued my thoughts until I felt I had it all under control.

"Now, Lord," I said, "since the thing is settled, I would like to ask some questions, if I may?"

"Go ahead and ask," the Lord didn't even sound annoyed, which I expected Him to be.

"This is Your ministry, right?" I began.

"That it is and don't you forget it," the Lord said. "And I give it and take it as I will," He continued.

"So, are you taking it from me?" I asked.

"No," the Lord answered, "but it is important that any servant of mine is willing to give back to Me what is entrusted to him or her. I give people dreams to follow, but there comes a time when they must hand back the dream."

"Is this what's happening right now with You and me?" I asked.

"No," the Lord said. "You wish to quit and I will let you and give you an easier task."

"Who will do the work?" I asked sadly.

"Don't worry about it. I'll find someone else. The work will be done. Remember it is My ministry. It will not die." The Lord answered clearly.

"Can I ask You something else?" I said, fighting tears.

"You may ask as much as you wish. I am not angry at you," the Lord reassured me.

"Jesus," I pondered, "Betty and I are teaching many Hebrew word pictures to help us western Christians to visualize spiritual concepts. My favorite Hebrew picture has always been the word *trust*. Hebrew scholars say it is the picture of a baby cuddled in a mother's arms. Now, in my imagination, I substitute the baby with a black sheep. I see myself as the stupid little lamb and You are the Shepherd. I have tried so often to jump into Your arms. I try so hard to trust. Are You carrying me or not? What has gone wrong?"

In the hum of the motor and the oppressive heat of the noonday the Lord spoke so clearly that I thought Betty could hear Him too.

"I have been carrying you for a long time, little lamb. If I hadn't you wouldn't be here any longer. It's not My holding you that wears you down. You are holding onto Me like a frightened child who is afraid of being dropped. I shall never let you fall, or drop you, My child, I love You!"

My tears rolled like a river and Betty looked with obvious concern, but she never said a word. She watched the road and I wept. I could feel my hands hurt from holding on so tightly. I looked down into my lap and my knuckles shone white. My hands were cramped into fists.

I opened my hands to relax and said. "Lord, *why* am I so afraid? Why am I clinging to You so desperately?"

"Almost everybody you have ever trusted on the human level, since you were a child, has let you down. You have been dropped, rejected, and betrayed so often that you simply expect it. Even death can be interpreted as abandonment. Your mama left you as a baby. Your foster mother came home to Me. The only father you ever had was the first president of the ministry. He died on you after a short time of beautiful friendship with him. You have been disappointed by staff members you trusted completely, people promised to come to work for you and broke their promises; your chlidren are caught in loyalty conflicts. You equate complete trust with terrible pain at the end. You have never believed that you are good enough to lead this ministry, and some day I would find someone better and *I* would drop you, too," the Lord explained slowly, carefully and so very lovingly. "You know you couldn't handle My rejection," the Lord continued. "So you are trying to prepare yourself for it by quitting first. It's not the heat and the hard travel or the financial squeeze that wear you down. It is a fear that you have carried within you since babyhood."

I commanded that fear to leave immediately in the name of Jesus. I also did much thinking and meditating for many long quiet hours and miles until we arrived home.

No other insight has ever affected me as deeply as this. It helped me to put the puzzle of my life together as never before. I could suddenly see reasons for some of my behavior, but I also understood many of the Lord's words in a new way.

The Lord and I talked freely again and I listened a lot. I also asked for forgiveness because I had such a hard time trusting Him. It should be the easiest thing in the world to trust Him, why was I so slow to learn?

I suddenly remembered a story I had heard on a tape which had moved me deeply, but I had forgotten about it. The Lord brought it back to my remembrance to make a point.

A successful faith healer found himself stricken by tuberculosis of the skin. He prayed, believed, claimed healing — and got worse. The pain was so unbearable that he was delirious for most of the time. Whenever he regained consciousness, he prayed and praised God and claimed healing again. One day he came out of his delirium to hear the nurses whisper softly. They talked about his only having hours to live. Before slipping back into the medicated fog of pain and confusion, his soul cried silently out to the Lord: "Jesus," he said, "I tried to believe You but I am dying. I don't believe You anymore. I can't do it any longer. All I can do is crawl into Your arms and ask You to hold me. I have come to the end...!"

A month later the man was out of the hospital healed and preaching again. He had a better message, for God had taught him a new formula for trust.

God had to teach me a few new things, too. We settled several issues for good and, hopefully, for always.

For the first time I accepted with certainty that the Lord had called me permanently to this ministry, I was not just an interim or a substitute until God could fill the position with a more capable person. I might *never* understand why He called me but the Lord seemed to say that this was His concern and responsibility and not mine. A clay pot may not question its maker why he formed the vessel for a certain purpose. It simply serves as designed.

The next thing I wondered about was why the Lord waited so long to show me my hidden paralyzing fear. I did not know that I carried it or I would have begun to resist it long before now.

Jesus showed me that growth and maturation takes time. Head knowledge comes long before true understanding of the heart. If He had shown it to me before I was ready, I might have never grasped the depth of it. We can talk about a spiritual principle, teach it, even try to live by it, but we have to grow step by step into His wisdom, and often it takes rain and storm to advance.

All sunshine makes a desert, I could look out the window of the motor home and see it. The parched land pleaded for a good rainstorm. Well, my storm was over, at least for the time being.

I made some solemn promises and had some specific

requests. By God's grace, I would serve Him as He saw fit to the end of my days. The ministry was His but if He chose me as the earthen vessel to carry it, I was willing to lead out and accept certain responsibilities connected with that leadership.

Realizing that a fear which had lodged in my subconscious all my life would return over and over again, I asked the Lord to point it out whenever I didn't recognize its nature.

"Whenever I cling to You for dear life, will You please show me?" I said to the Lord. "I will do my best to let go since You are holding me always."

Yes, I finally have found the missing link. The last puzzle piece is in and the picture is complete for me. The perfect trust I am still praying for is not the Lord's work alone. It is a gift of heaven, but I decide how *much* to trust!

I knew before I arrived home that I had to make a clear decision whether I would hold on or let go. Both' ways Jesus would carry me home. I was sure of that. It might be easier to cling to Him, hide my face in His bosom, and turn my back on a cruel world. But if I let go, He could use me some more. He might even put me down sometimes and ask me to walk with Him, or even before Him.

As long as I hang on to Him in fear, I am saying: "If He slays me, yet will I trust Him." But when I let go I find a new assurance: I know that I know that I know that He will *never* let me drop. He holds me because He promised to, not because I deserve it or earned His love! It does not even matter if I understand His words or His ways with me. If it rains we both get wet. If I hurt, Jesus hurts with me. If it storms He breaks the wind for me. I don't need to hold on, He is holding me. He *is* able to hold (2 Timothy 1:12).

My joy is back. It's not my honeymoon rejoicing of the past. It is a deeper joy, a new assurance that I know He is always as near as I want Him to be. Even through the last two confusing and unstable years He was there all the time.

June, Beginning of Summer/*Monday*

So much has happened since I last recorded, I better not wait until the end of the year. I might forget some of the special moments.

I did not tell in my previous entry what happened after we returned home from our tour. The retreat took place and I did face the annual board meeting. I even gave my farewell and thank-you speech that I had memorized, but only in the context of my quiet and tearful disclosure about my struggles and final rededication to my job. We all gave a deep sigh of relief and began to lay prayerful plans for the coming year.

New things have emerged. The year before last had taught me to teach the book of Job. In the recent retreat I was able to teach about the life of King David, Israel's sweet singer and greatest monarch. The Lord showed me how David's life was overshadowed with a spirit of rejection from childhood on. He had to overcome it to find that complete trust in his great Shepherd.

People told me it was our best retreat ever, in spite of untold difficulties. It almost seemed that hell had doubled its efforts to overturn my newfound commitment. The caretaker of the Christian retreat center quit just a week or two before our retreat date. The kitchen crew got lost and we had a camp full of hungry people wondering and waiting for the first evening meal. Quarters were cramped and the November weather too hot during the day and too cold at night. Through it all I determined to "let go." "If this is Your retreat, it's Your problem, not mine," I would repeatedly remind Jesus when I felt my stomach and knuckles tighten. To my amazement I watched every difficulty turn into a blessing.

I had leveled with the audience about our various problems and everybody pitched in, quickly, cheerfully, and without grumbling or putting the blame anywhere; everyone tried to help us and each other. The closeness could be felt and joy prevailed. I was so overwhelmed I did not even lose my composure when we found out that we had lost all six recordings on our master tapes through unintentional human error by the staff. The problems of the retreat had taxed them to the limit and I certainly could understand their haste. I assured them that God could bring good out of this calamity, too. Betty and I did something we had never done before. We re-recorded the retreat messages in our living room, without audience reaction of any kind. We did not know if we could do it but we found out that Jesus could, and He did!

When we finished, I looked up and said, "Lord, I am slowly learning that I can do all things through You. You simply always find a way where we can see none. This re-recording looked hopeless to us."

"There will always be a way," the Lord assured me. "Remember I AM the way."

His words have stuck by us in the eventful months of this year. Looking at the way the ministry is still situated, things have not changed too much, at least not outwardly. Finances are still tight but we are slowly stabilizing. Payroll has been on time since the retreat. Several larger gifts permitted us to buy a tape duplicator and make office improvements that help us to save money in the long run. We have not been able to resume our TV or radio programs. But, looking at our schedule, we don't have time to do it right now anyway.

Shortly after I had reenlisted for the Lord's work, we received a letter from a US chaplain stationed in Turkey. He inquired if Betty and I could come and serve the chaplain communities of all the US military bases in Turkey. He had heard us speak at one of the Air Force bases in America and found out that our overseas tour would take us to Israel in April. Would we be willing to

spend the month of March with the US armed forces?
Would we! Even my staff was surprised by my ecstasy
until I explained that I had prayed for years to be sent to
Turkey. When I served our US bases all over Europe in
1977 I had been told about the hardship assignment of
our American forces in Turkey. During the Carter
administration these US bases did not even exist in
congressional records and our troops often found themselves in deepest trouble, with little support from the
homeland and vicious hostility from the host land.
Nobody visited them. They were more forgotten than
our brave boys on the Korean demarcation line. I
pleaded with various officials of the armed forces to let
me go, but nothing happened. I asked the Lord to open
the doors but nothing came of it for five years. Now
Jesus was answering.

The devil moved in to scare us the moment the letter
arrived. Turkey is not a place for two lone unprotected
American women to visit. We would not travel under
the auspices of the US government, time was too short
to cut all the red tape involved. We would use our group
ticket to fly into Israel via Switzerland, but fly
Turkish Airlines into and all around Turkey. It sounded
foreboding. Little did we know how true our premoni-
tions would prove.

One fear raised its ugly head immediately. How
would the ministry manage to pay the current bills with
us gone for two months, at a time when we are generally
at the height of our speaking tour here in America? Not
one of us could ignore the fact that these US tours were
not only our bread and butter but the means to print,
help the needy, and put Bibles behind the Iron Curtain.

Talk about resisting the devil! The Lord kept His
promise and reminded me, whenever I began to cling to
Him with anxious questions of "what if," that finances
were His problem. Our protection was His responsibility also.

Just before we left, the office received a long distance
phone call from our chaplain friend in Turkey. All the

American teachers employed at the US bases were
having their annual teachers' convention in Izmir, our
first stop. The American ambassador to Turkey was to
be their keynote speaker. He had to cancel. Could Hansi
take his place? The office manager assured him I would
fill in.

I swallowed hard and had a long talk with the Lord.
Jet lag would be a harsh thing for the first few days and
I would be speaking two days after our arrival in
Turkey.

Things didn't go right from the moment we had to
board Turkish aircraft. We left late and landed in the
middle of the night in Istanbul. Our hired and paid for
taxi was not waiting. We finally found someone who
spoke English and got another taxi. We paid again and
rolled into the night. Betty had been in Turkey before
and remembered that the airport was way out in
nowhere and it would take a while to get to the city and
to our hotel. The drive seemed endless with no city in
sight.

"I am glad Jesus is along," I whispered. "That rough-
looking Turkish driver could be taking us anywhere, hit
us over the head and vanish with our purses and
luggage into the darkness."

The city finally appeared and we were dropped off at
the American hotel we had requested. What a relief!

The next day we took a sightseeing tour through
Istanbul. As a child I had been taught about the terrible
Turkish wars, the sultans, the pashas, and the incredible wealth of the Turkish emperors. One has to see the
largest emerald in the world, diamonds and rubies as
big as hens' eggs, and thousands of other precious
stones in crowns, saber sheaths and handles, thrones,
utensils and garments; I cannot adequately describe
them in words.

It was a cold wet day and my body shivered, but so did
my soul. Turkish history is a record of massacre, the
butchery of countless millions, inhuman cruelty, and
ruthless thirst for blood and conquest. Thousands were

tortured or died for every jewel glistening behind
museum windows or on display in the palace. I shall
never forget when the guide stopped at a Moslem
cemetery because we wanted to take pictures. A mauso-
leum not usually open to the public caught our eye. The
doors were ajar and we peaked in. A Turkish caretaker
was dusting. Our guide slipped him some coins and he
let us walk in, but permitted no picture taking. We
promised and "looked only" at the ornate sarcophagus.
One of their most famous sultans rested here. The mini-
dome was covered with royal blue velvet and shiny
pieces of glass shimmered like stars in the dim light. I
made a remark about the intensity of the polished glass
reflectors and the guide chuckled softly. "Excuse me,
madam, these are diamonds, every one of them."

I kept my remarks to myself after that. My heart
rebelled and ached. This one burial place contained
enough wealth to lift the poverty of every beggar on the
streets of Istanbul, and there are hundreds of such
places, some bigger and more decorated. The value of
the Turkish crown jewels alone cannot even be esti-
mated in our modern world. They are priceless.

We flew into Izmir, known in New Testament times as
Smyrna, and the chaplain welcomed us. He handed us
our week's schedule, typed out in minute detail, military
style.

"Please let me give you some personal briefing and
advice in addition to the schedule," he said as we drove
to our hotel. "Turkey had a military coup two years ago
and is under strict dictatorship. You will see Turkish
soldiers everywhere. One of the laws passed by the new
head of state is called an insult law. Under it, any
person who feels insulted by someone may walk up to
any Turkish soldier and tell him about it. The accused is
taken to jail without further witnesses and with no
trial."

Betty and I laughed, it sounded so absurd. "Please,
don't think it is a joke," the chaplain advised us
seriously. "We have Americans in jail because they

didn't believe it and we have not been able to get them out."

We promised to be careful and checked into the Turkish hotel. Our room was on the top floor and we could overlook part of the bay, an open space around a monument, and the corner where two main streets crossed. The traffic was hair-raising — honking cars, carts pulled by animals or pushed by people, bicycles, motorcycles, and everything else imaginable.

Betty and I had some time before we would be picked up for dinner and we watched the stop and go of the never-ending flow of vehicles and pedestrians. On each side of the street stood a Turkish soldier, machine gun in his hands.

"Now I know why Turkey appears so different," Betty said. "When I was here ten years ago they had no military government. I never heard of an insult law then. I still wonder if it is as serious as the chaplain says. I cannot see how it could work among the Turks, they are the most hot-tempered men I know of when they get into a dispute."

We didn't have to wait too long until we watched one car skid right into another vehicle. The corner had no traffic light. Betty laughed softly and said: "Now, let's watch and see what will happen."

The two drivers got out and obviously glared at each other. They looked around. The soldiers stood at every corner with pointed guns, motionless. The two gentlemen embraced each other, kissed each other's cheek, went back to their vehicles, untangled them, and drove off.

Betty was speechless! When she could finally talk about it, she said: "I thought I understood when you talk about inner and outer control in your freedom lectures. I see a new meaning. What we just saw was order by outer control." She chuckled and looked at me. "I have been thinking. Do you remember the wild ride we had in Istanbul when we hired a taxi to drive us around to take more pictures?"

I laughed and nodded. "My dear, I shall never forget
that taxi ride as long as I live. The driver ran through
every red light in the city except one. I did much
praying while I held my breath. These are the times
when I know Jesus is especially with us. I even asked
the man why we stopped when we did. He grinned and
said in his poor English: 'Too many people killed here.
Five streets come together. Only light we sometimes
stop and look...' He looked around and screeched away
before the light changed, remember? I had my heart in
my throat!"

Betty said, "It seems that even in a dictatorship they
cannot control everything and so they let some things
slip. The people know where they must obey and when
they can get away with breaking a rule. Red traffic
lights can be outraced, but if there is a soldier at the
corner, people kiss in place of a customary loud, arm-
waving argument. Do you know that in America most
drivers stop at a stop sign or red light even if no other
car is on the road and no policeman in sight?"

I nodded. Yes, I had watched Betty herself drive at
two o'clock in the morning through a sleeping town
with rolled-up sidewalks, only one traffic light in the
middle of the village, no car or person in sight and she
waited patiently until the light turned green before pro-
ceeding. Things can actually get funny anywhere in the
good ol' USA when a red light malfunctions and
remains red. I have observed, several times, how Americans line up for blocks honking their horns impatiently
because the car at the red light does not move but waits
and waits and waits!

Talking about inner control of freedom versus outer
control to keep order in a country! We saw much and
made many mental notes. We learned to talk freely only
within the privacy of our hotel room or when we entered
buildings on the US base. Betty would murmur under
her breath, "I hate those guns," when we walked across
any street. We could feel the eyes of the watchful
Turkish soldiers and the holes of their machine guns

burn on our backs. They never did us any harm and I was determined to keep it that way.

"Please, don't even murmur," I would admonish Betty, the all-American kid. I knew dictatorship and how to submit wordlessly. I hated it, but I knew I could tolerate it for a month. Betty bristled, she felt so insulted by the human mistrust and the strict rules the military government imposed on everybody, including foreigners. Her favorite descriptive word is "stupid." Anything she does not like she calls a stupid thing to do or to be.

"Please, park that word until we leave Turkey," I said seriously. "You can pick it up in Israel again. The Israeli soldiers carry their guns on their shoulders, not in their hands with their fingers on the trigger. You can shout it from the housetops in America if you wish."

Yes, the shadows of my past came back and tried to scare me. When it was time to give the keynote address to the American teachers, I wondered if I should change my theme and talk about something else instead of freedom.

The meeting was in the penthouse of a Turkish hotel, and below the windows stood Turkish militia with guns in hand. "I am letting go, dear Jesus," I said. "You speak through me, although this is a secular convention."

Freedom was obviously the most important topic to the Lord. He and I did not soften the message, and at the end I watched my fellow Americans stand and clap, and many tears rolled. I saw even male teachers and principals wipe their eyes. I was surrounded, hugged, squeezed, and kissed by so many I felt dazed. Before the chaplain escorted us out, he announced that we would visit every US base in Turkey. I had invitations to speak in every school on every base as we waved goodbye to the teachers.

We came to serve and did not expect any returns but we got so much, we shall never be the same again. The Lord blessed the meetings and the love and appreciation for our coming often moved us to tears. We visited and ate in the homes of our service people. We listened to their stories and hardships — so that America might stay free. So often we forget those who watch and defend our national freedom. The chaplains in Turkey were dedicated and eager to encourage spiritual growth in the Lord. They and their families outdid themselves to make our stay worthwhile for our benefit, too.

Betty had hoped I could see some of the sites of the seven New Testament churches in Asia Minor, which she had visited before. Our chaplain friend took us to six of the seven and we saw several other places mentioned in connection with the Apostle Paul. It is hard to describe the awe one feels when walking in the footsteps of the Apostles.

Betty gave a devotional at a church outing which took a whole busload of service families to Miletus, the place where Paul met the elders from Ephesus as recorded in Acts 20. I remember that assignment so well because I wondered if Betty would be able to speak. Her allergies had gone wild since our arrival in Turkey, and she had a hard time climbing stairs or even going up a hill. However, she did speak, and with great emphasis and conviction. The service people loved her and her ability to bring stories or places to life. By the time she finished we could see Paul standing at the now vanished seashore and the elders weeping because they would never see his face again.

We did the same when we left a few days later. We had no idea if we would see any of those dear people ever again and we hated to leave, but the next place already had our activities planned and announced.

I shall not waste space or time to describe the frustrations and trials of flying Turkish Airlines from place to place. Our kind chaplain stayed with us and his helpful wife had packed some food for us. I shall be forever grateful for their thoughtfulness. We waited for half a day at the Izmir airport to board the small plane to Ankara. I call such kinds of aggravations "the gnats of life," and these small things can be extremely draining and wearisome.

The Turkish authorities didn't bother to explain why the aircraft didn't leave. It was sitting outside the gate in full view. Other English speaking travelers assured us that it could be either fog or rain somewhere en route. Turkish Airlines don't operate in bad weather. Or they had mechanical trouble. A few days before, a plane scheduled for Istanbul had a defective part, someone told me very quietly. A high military officer was on board, so they simply removed the needed part from the engine of the Ankara plane. The flight to Istanbul went out; the Ankara plane sat on the runway and did not leave until the following day. The passengers were not informed until evening that no flight would go out; they had waited the entire day.

Fortunately, we did leave the same day and arrived in Ankara before evening. I had hoped the new place would be easier on Betty's breathing. Hers is a chemical allergy, we had discovered, and Izmir's exhaust fumes under our hotel windows did her no good. Smoking is another of her aggravaters and Turkey is covered with a blue haze of tobacco smoke everywhere people move or live. Turkish boys begin smoking at the age of six or even younger. Everybody smokes, it seems. Life expectancy is way below the age of sixty we found out. Many people die young from tobacco-related diseases.

Turkish Airlines has designated one side of the aircraft as non-smoking, across the small aisle the smokers billow anything they wish — cigars, pipes, foul-smelling weed. Betty's nose was closed and her eyes were swollen before we ever landed.

My hopes vanished into a yellow-brown fog when the plane circled over Ankara. We found out later that Turkey's capital vies with Mexico City for the title of the most polluted city on earth. I had never seen a pollution cover as dense and visible as the blanket of soft coal smoke covering the entire city of Ankara. We drove right into it when an army van picked us up and brought us to the place we would stay for the entire week. It was a US military guesthouse in the middle of the city and in the heaviest smog area. We were dropped off, handed a key and told when to be ready next morning. The chaplain was polite but distant and very busy. What a difference from base to base, I thought.

We unpacked in silence. We had a kitchen, food in the refrigerator, and a sitting room available. The weather was still freezing and central steam heat made the rooms stifling hot. We opened windows and watched the black smoke billow out of every chimney below the high building we stayed in. We could taste the sulfur, and blew black soot out of our noses as we tried to get rid of the congestion and smell in our nostrils.

We tried to sleep. "Lord," I pleaded, "please do a miracle. Betty will never survive this week. I remember the night a few weeks ago when she nearly choked in California. You know about it, Lord. We had meetings in a town and stayed at a farm surrounded by blossoming almond trees. They sprayed the groves while we were there and Betty couldn't breath any longer. Our friends couldn't find a doctor in town, we prayed around Betty's bedside, and she got better. She even taught Sunday School the next morning. Lord, please do it again."

I must have fallen into a fitful sleep when I heard Betty wheeze: "Help me, please."

I jumped out of bed with both feet and felt my mouth go dry with fear. I turned on the light, Betty sat in her bed and fought for breath.

"Pray me through, help me pray," she said. "I can't fight it alone."

I knew she was seriously in trouble because Betty will suffer great discomfort and go to any length not to disturb my sleep. If she felt the need to waken me, she had to be at panic level. "What is it?" I said. "Are you getting as bad as the last time?"

"No," she said between wheezing, "it's not as bad as it was, not yet. It is the fear that it might get as bad or worse, and we are trapped. We don't know anybody here, we have no way of calling someone for help or special prayer. I feel an evil power attacking me and I can't take it on alone."

"You don't have to, Betty," I said. "There are three of us. The Lord is here and I'll stay with you and pray you through. Let me just open the window and I'll be right back."

We felt the cool night breeze and I took her hand and we took turns praying. We commanded the power of Satan to leave in Jesus' name and take all his hellish spirits of fear with him. Betty's attack lasted for hours but it never got as bad as in California. By the time she could breathe without a struggle, her hand felt limp and her skin was wet and clammy.

"Betty," I said, "if you can't handle this horrible smog, I will put you on the next plane and send you home. Your survival is more important than that you come with me."

Betty spoke very quietly: "This decision is for me to make, not for you. I appreciate your concern; don't take me wrong, but it's just between the Lord and me whether I go or stay. I believe He brought us both here to serve. Unless you take me out on a stretcher, I shall not leave. Jesus can either change the air or touch my chest, and if He does neither, I serve Him anyway. Right now, we both need some sleep so we can meet our schedule tomorrow."

I crawled back under my cover and listened to her breathing. She had fallen asleep immediately and was sounding fine. Her wheezing was gone.

Betty's severe bronchial problems improved from day to day in the thickest pollution Ankara had suffered in months. The smog was caused by heavy fog which trapped the coal smoke over the city. Betty taught her Bible classes, climbed stairs and hills, went sightseeing, and breathed through all of it. She considers Ankara not only one of the turning points for her longtime respiratory problems, but she believes that it was her supreme lesson of complete trust. She had to decide if she would go home defeated by a devastating fear (and I have been told that the anxiety of suffocating is one of the ugliest sensations known to humans), or be sure that she knew of Jesus' love even if there was no instant miracle.

She decided to trust Him completely, and our stay in Ankara became a time of blessings and joyful victories. We hated to leave and even became good friends with the busy chaplain and his family. Some of the military people are such good friends we are still corresponding with them.

Two happenings stand out in my mind when I remember our busy schedule in Ankara. One women's group had scheduled a visit to a Turkish bath far out in the country, past the surrounding mountains of Ankara. The bus stuttered over rough roads in heavy fog and we finally arrived at the natural sulfur hot spring which had been made into a public bath. I begged to be excused and so did Betty. We wandered into the village instead, while the other American women had a good soaking. On our long ride back, the fog had lifted and we looked out at hill after hill of the most monotonous, treeless, brownish, rocky land area we had ever seen—very few villages, some stubble fields with a few patches of dirty melting snow, and a waving horizon of endless, clean-shaven, brown earth, vast and full of loneliness.

Betty said, "Do you know what you are looking at?"

I said, "You mean this strange landscape we have been driving through for hours?"

"We are in the midst of Galatia, my dear," Betty said almost reverently. "This is the area the Apostle Paul crisscrossed to preach the gospel."

We could almost see it! A lone human form, perhaps leading a small donkey loaded with a few belongings, walking, walking, climbing up and down mountains, so far between villages, so tiresome, so few places to rest or find a drink. Oh, Saul of Tarsus, you have come a long way from your days as a Pharisee!

We both had tears in our eyes and didn't talk much for the rest of the bus ride.

The other special occasion was my speech to the American high school assembly. I had been informed that Turkish students attended the US base school, too. Some American men had married Turkish women with children from former Turkish marriages. Other high Turkish government officials wanted their children to learn English and paid tuition to send their youngsters to the American school, which had a high reputation for scholastic achievement, and excellent discipline.

One American high ranking officer assured me that he would be at the school meeting. He also announced that he admired Turkish rigid discipline strongly and thought America needed what Turkey had.

"Lord," I prayed and relaxed my tense knuckles, "if You want me to speak on freedom, I need superhuman wisdom or I end up in a Turkish prison the moment I walk off the US base. And I am not so sure every American will be cheering for me either."

I started my message by defining for the Turkish students in the crowd how America's democracy works and that freedom always demands individual inner control. (The American students listened carefully, too.) Then, I explained outer control of dictatorship. I described the need of it whenever inner control failed. Having informed myself on Turkish history before I spoke, I showed them how Ataturk had tried to give Turkey democracy and used the Western world as his model. He made one great miscalculation when he destroyed the people's personal religion. Turkey became a godless country where Moslem traditions were only strong enough to make the masses fatalistic and with no hope for life to come. Everyone tried to get the most out of this life. So graft, corruption, political swindle and terrorism got out of hand. Two years ago a military leader cared enough for this country to take over and restore law and order in Turkey. Such a man could be called a "benevolent dictator," I said. Turkey needed him and people are grateful that he came and they can walk the streets in safety again. American service people are just as glad. Two years ago they left the US base only at their own risk. Many people were shot at a dark street corner just because someone needed a pair of boots or a pack of cigarettes. Things are different now. Terrorism is almost nonexistent because offenders of the existing marshal law are shot on the spot. Law-abiding citizens are not threatened by these harsh law enforcements, so life is better for them.

Then I spoke to the American students: "Young people," I said, "you might miss the carefree life of a teenager in the USA. There is no McDonald's or an ice cream parlor around the corner in which to hang out. You are hesitant to form strong peer group ties because you move so often. But you have one great gift: You can see and understand how the rest of the world lives and what privileges we have in America. Everything on earth has a price, freedom does too.

"With freedom comes the responsibility to choose. And you know from your young experience that America has only two ways to go: We either discipline ourselves and keep America free or we let go of our inner controls and hope to get a benevolent dictator to restore America's law and order. But we could also end up with a tyrant who would destroy freedom completely.

"I pray that some of you will become the future leaders of America, for you had to mature fast living so far away from home. When you return to America, please help me spread the message that freedom is worth keeping and even fighting for.

"May God bless Turkey and may God bless our beloved free America!"

The student body exploded into a standing ovation, the Turks and Americans stood and clapped together. They whistled and some of the young people and several teachers cried.

The American high officer avoided my eyes when he

shook my hand. "You gave us much to think about," he said, and walked off.

I had a hard time getting away from the students. They wanted to ask hundreds of questions. I told them to go back and ask their teachers and have a good class discussion. I would love to have been a little mouse so I could have listened without being observed.

Not every American leader needs to think through the concepts of freedom. Of the many high ranking men we met, up to a two-star general, one tall, gray-haired officer with a booming voice stands out in my memory. We had to wait in his office to be introduced and I found a poem framed on his desk. I asked him for it and he gave me a copy. I was so impressed. It sums up my philosophy about God, America, and freedom, too. I see it completely compatible with my views on Christian principles of love and mercy.

> *War is an ugly thing,*
>   *But not the ugliest of things;*
> *The decayed and degraded state*
>   *Of moral and patriotic feeling*
>   *which*
> *Thinks that nothing is worth war*
>   *Is much worse.*
> *A man who has nothing*
>   *For which he is willing to fight;*
> *Nothing he cares about more*
>   *Than his own personal safety;*
> *Is a miserable creature*
>   *Who has no chance of being*
>   *free,*
> *Unless made and kept so*
>   *By the exertions of better men*
>   *than himself.*

>   *—Author Unknown*

We don't know who wrote this poem, but I know who made the following statement:

> *They that give up essential Liberty*
> *to obtain a little temporary safety*
> *deserve neither Liberty or safety.*

—Benjamin Franklin

New Year's Day/*Sunday*

Another Sunday, another New Year's day, just a few months later, but it seems like a small eternity in some ways. So many things have happened around me, but the greatest change has taken place within me.

The past year alone has been a mind boggler with the many unusual episodes and so much new learning for Betty and me.

We went to Turkey to serve but that one month by itself has influenced so many of our activities since we returned. It is not just a flippant saying that we shall never be the same again. We simply cannot be the same again, ever, and we shall never forget certain high points.

The last week of our visit to the US bases took us to the south of Turkey, right to the shores of the Mediterranean Sea.

Two Biblical places that even Betty had never seen had our interest and attention. When the chaplain picked us up at the small Turkish airport, I stretched out my hand and said, "Hi, we are Hansi and Betty and we want to see ancient Antioch and Tarsus."

He laughed good-naturedly and said, "OK! We already got the message that you are eager to see both places. We shall show them to you."

We had some very good meetings and a fine time with our Americans in Adana. One chaplain drove us and some other ladies to Antioch. Of all the historic sites I have ever seen, no other place has engraved itself as deeply in my memory as the cave that became the refuge and shelter for the first Christian church. It was at Antioch that the believers were first called Christians.

The church is a hole in the side of a steep mountain slope and can be seen a long way off. When we entered

the cave itself and stood on the same stones where
perhaps Peter or Paul or some of the other early church
leaders might have stood about two thousand years
ago, I suddenly understood why money was never a
problem for the Lord.

"Not by might nor by power, but by My Spirit," I
thought. The birthplace of world missions began in a
cave that had hidden tunnels in the back, through
which the Christians could escape when they were
attacked either by the Romans or by other fanatics.

Hardships did not stop these people, poverty became
relative. They set aside Paul and Barnabas for God's
work. They also collected love gifts for the suffering
church in Jerusalem.

On the way back our eyes scanned the massive
mountain ranges. Betty pointed to a deep cut between
steep cliffs and said softly, "The Cilician Gates. That's
how Paul entered Turkey to reach Galatia."

We drove many miles and returned greatly satisfied
but physically exhausted. Driving on Turkish highways is more dangerous than flying. The chaplain told
us after we were safely back that the highway is known
as "the death road." Every day someone is killed, since
most Turks drive fatalistically, which is another word
for reckless driving.

Well, things haven't changed much since Paul's time,
I thought. He found himself "in journeyings often, in
perils of waters, in perils of robbers, in perils by mine
own countrymen, in perils by the heathen, in perils in
the city, in perils in the wilderness, in perils in the sea,
in perils among false brethren; in weariness and pain-
fulness, in watchings often, in hunger and thirst, in
fastings often, in cold and nakedness" (2 Corinthians
11:26-27) on most of his travels.

Tarsus had a surprise for us. Not until we walked in
the old garden, which supposedly contains Paul's well,
did it dawn on me that Jesus had prepared His great
apostle to the Gentiles from birth on. Saul of Tarsus
was a Jew by heritage but every citizen of Tarsus had

been given Roman citizenship as a reward because the city had given loyal service to the Roman emperor during a time of crisis.

The orthodox family of Saul lived, no doubt, in the Jewish quarter of the city, but from childhood on he learned to mingle with Gentiles, speak their language and dialect and understand their thinking. Perhaps some of his playmates or teenage friends were non-Jewish, much to the consternation of his well-to-do super-orthodox parents. One can only guess, but I, of course, let my imagination wander freely and we literally walked in Paul's footsteps.

Nothing happens by accident when God has His hands in it. None of His children are ever subject to chance or happenstance, no matter how small or big the incident.

I remember one specific American serviceman who might have forgotten by now what he said to us just before we had to leave. He looked a little bit like my son, so very young and vulnerable, and he meant what he said as a compliment. He pumped my hand and had a lonely look in his eyes while he tried to joke. "Thanks, ladies, for coming to us. You are the second visitors we ever had. The others were the Dallas Cowgirls, and they came and left the same day."

I looked at Betty. "Not bad to be compared with or follow such a famous beauty group!" I smiled but my heart felt heavy. Why must our soldiers be so lonely and forgotten most of the time? Unless a tragedy puts a certain spot on earth in the news, America forgets her lonely fighters and defenders of freedom. I pray that Betty and I can help to bring a change. I shall not forget the "little" incident and the one sentence which lodged itself into my heart.

Once more, before we left Turkey, the priceless gift of freedom in America burned itself into our memory because we watched the absence of it at the Istanbul airport.

We did arrive, after a late departure from Adana due

to a rainstorm, in time to catch our connecting morning
flight into Greece. We breathed a prayer of relief and
rushed up to the ticket counter of the Greek airline, only
to be informed that they had gone on strike.

Our American boys had told us that the initials of the
Turkish Airlines, THY, stands for "They Hate You."
Well, the other airlines of that part of the world should
all carry similar letters, perhaps TDC for "They Don't
Care."

Nobody showed any concern or sympathy for the
stranded travelers, some of them much worse off than
we were. European vacationers with prepaid hotel reservations in various countries found themselves without
a connection and no place to stay in or go to.

Our great concern was the fact that we had to meet
our American tour in Israel by the end of the week, only
three days away. No flying into Israel either, we found
out, the only scheduled flight for the week had been
cancelled.

The Lord had to pull a few strings and thanks to Him
and Swiss Airlines we joined with our tour group in
Zurich. Thank God also for credit cards. It cost us much
extra money to leave our benevolent dictatorship behind and breathe free air again, but we knew we could
pay it off slowly and gladly.

The last hours in Turkey became the hardest of our
entire trip. We were on our own, no helpful chaplain
around to see us through. Nobody had packed a loving
lunch because we expected to be in our hotel in Athens
by noon. Before we left Adana a dear Turkish lady who
had married an American officer had admonished us
not to eat or drink in the Istanbul airport. "I thought I
knew what to order," she said, "being born in Istanbul,
but my husband and I got terribly sick the last time we
flew out."

I assured her we had no reason to do so because we
would stop over only to catch a plane to Athens and
then on to Tel Aviv in Israel.

We waited until evening to board our Swiss aircraft.

The agent did help us by locking our big luggage away so that we had only our handbags and our coats to carry. The smoky air in the waiting hall could have been cut with a knife. I suggested to Betty that we go across the street and sit in a small park and wait it out. I had a pint-size thermos filled with water from the US base and a few crackers. The weather had finally turned warm and we sat on our coats on the grass. We didn't dare sit on a bench. Only men sat on them, smoking and staring relentlessly at us. We knew better than to look back. We had been warned that a woman looking fully into a man's face in the Turkish way of life extended an invitation. American women had been raped, before the coup made the streets safe again, by Turkish men who claimed they had been given permission by the woman's look.

We kept our eyes down. Our books were in the big suitcase. We sipped the water, one swallow at a time, nibbled some crackers and let the hours drag by. Suddenly Betty's face brightened. "I know what we can do," she smiled. "Our little tape recorder is in my flight bag. I put new batteries in before we came. And I also have our favorite tape handy."

The Lord spoke urgently, "No!"

"No, Betty," I said, "the Lord is vetoing clearly."

By then she had obviously received the same message. She looked at me. "Why can't we fill our waiting hours with listening to some music?"

"It's Christian music, Betty," I said quietly. "Remember, the law of the land which does not permit any Christian meetings on Turkish property. Two people are already considered a 'meeting.' So if we begin playing softly in a public place like this, we can be arrested. If a Turkish passerby stops to listen or talk to us, we are guilty of proselytizing. My friend, you have much to learn about the way the rest of the world lives."

We sat very quietly for the remaining long, oppressive hours, while people leered, frowned, snickered or shook their heads about the two foreign old women waiting without a male escort in a public park.

The experience left us emotionally shaken and most grateful to the Lord that His protective cover was back over us. It also took me a few days to stabilize my low blood sugar and to stop my physical shaking. His loving care was so obvious and our joy complete when we met our tour group in Zurich and left for Israel to celebrate Easter morning at the Garden Tomb in Jerusalem.

Yes, He is risen and because He lives we live also, and He came to set us free from fear and bondage of any kind.

* * * * * * * *

Betty has caught a new vision about freedom this year. She has always been more aware of it than the average American who was born in America, but now she has given it a lot of thought.

Right after we returned from overseas we picked up our interrupted speaking tour across America and we knew we had turned a corner with fear also when our motor home almost went over a steep cliff on our way home. As the windstorm howled, we prayed and Betty held onto the steering wheel so tightly that her hands were swollen for days afterward. But Jesus kept us free of fear. Satan tried his utmost to wear us down. We had ministerial opposition, snowstorms in May, upsetting counseling sessions with troubled people, and technical problems with our RV, a lot of unusual car trouble! Our fuel pump gave out twice! Colorado's altitude nearly did us in! We managed to roll the vehicle into a repair shop before it quit completely.

A friend came to transport us to a meeting in her community while the RV got fixed. She said it had been hard going. Her own minister had opposed our coming and everything that could go wrong had done so. She had come with a small truck so she could load our books, tapes, and suitcases. As she drove and talked, Betty and I both saw in the distance an object on the highway. When we got nearer, we looked in disbelief. A huge rattlesnake, several times the size of my arm, poised in the middle of the mountain road, coiled, ready to strike while its rattles buzzed.

The driver never saw the reptile. Betty and I looked at each other. "Lord," I prayed. "Satan is preparing for our coming and he put the snake there to scare us. He is striking at us as the snake did."

"Remember, I crushed the serpent's head," the Lord reassured me. "The victory is already won!"

Yes, we did see God's love win before the weekend was over. And we did get the motor home safely back. Jesus *is* Victor!

Betty did not have to struggle with fear when the Lord gave her the topic for our annual retreat this August. She simply thought that she didn't hear Jesus correctly. She got the topic of freedom for all six of her messages. I would speak on being alone and on another controversial topic: the Holy Spirit.

We both had long talks with the Lord. We asked the other to confirm what we had perhaps misunderstood.

"Freedom is her topic," Betty argued with the Lord, "Everybody knows it."

"She is the scholar; she explains the Biblical teachings on the Holy Spirit. And as for the other topic, Lord, it takes my heart blood to speak on that."

The Lord did not make a mistake and we had heard correctly. I could see why Betty had to speak on Christian freedom. Nobody could object to her teaching, she is all-American in heritage, she had a wonderful Christian upbringing and she showed us Biblical principles of freedom from the book of Galatians. It wasn't just experience alone. People can disagree with me for various reasons. It is hard to refute Betty's conclusions. Her teaching on the "Freedom Book" is sorely needed in the Christian community. Not only are evangelicals very often capable of shooting their own wounded, they are also guilty of denying each other personal freedom of choice, even in the Lord.

We teach about Jesus Christ who came to set us free.

And then we try to bind each other into the bondage of legalism, personal interpretation and denominational distinctives in the name of the same Christ. The longer I observe the American Protestant subculture, the more I believe that Satan has a heyday splitting us Christians by extreme beliefs.

When a woman comes to me for counsel during a retreat and tells me that her husband has a girlfriend but her minister has advised her that total submission will win the erring mate back, I have to pray for a composed spirit; I don't believe it. But since I know that people might see me biased as a divorced woman, I sometimes suggest that they talk to Betty. She has nothing to prove and stays more unruffled most of the time.

I have seen her walk into our room with sparks flying from her eyes. She considers it a Christian disgrace to teach our women that mindless submission is Biblical.

The New Testament does tell women to submit to their husbands, but it also tells husbands to love their wives as Christ loves the Church. He laid down His life for His bride. Which woman would not willingly submit to a husband with such unselfish protective love? But submit to unfaithfulness or other sins just to fit under an umbrella of authority, be it mate, parents, or any other boss?

Betty did some checking to find out what the words in the Bible mean. She told me that there are two words in Greek for *submit*. The first means to yield completely for your own good. But when Paul speaks of wives submitting to husbands he chooses a different word. His choice means to recognize authority, it is a military word. When an officer gives orders in a battle, the troops follow his instructions. In other words, Paul says, "Let the husband be the head of the house."

It is interesting that the Hebrew picture in the Old Testament goes even further. God created a "helpmate" for Adam. The literal Hebrew says, "a helper in front of him" or "against him." When the man makes the right choices she complements him. They compensate for each other's shortcomings. But when he does something wrong, she hinders him. Agreement is not always the best way "to help." The Jewish sages say, "A wife is neither man's shadow or a servant, but his other self, a 'helper' in a dimension beyond the capability of any other creature."

If the total woman has to park her brain and her own spiritual experience to meet her husband's or the church's demands, we are in the same boat as the Galatians were when Paul lamented, "I marvel that ye are so soon removed from him that called you into the grace of Christ unto another gospel" (Galatians 1:6).

Betty had just returned from the place where the Apostle's words had been directed so long ago, and she understood what Paul had given of himself to preach freedom.

Sometimes I do not only lose my cool when I watch husbands misuse Christianity to force their wives to tolerate sin, but I can get most upset when ministers lead their congregations like little dictators.

I shall never forget the time when one farmer's wife told me that she had to leave her home where she and her husband had raised their children, because he had begun to help a divorced neighbor lady and had fallen in love with her. Now he wanted his wife of many years out so that he could bring the new love in, and he would give her enough money to live in town in an apartment!

"Why would you want to give up your home?" I asked her.

"I don't want to," she cried. "But he threatens to build a new house right beside the farmhouse for her if I don't leave."

She wasn't sure she could handle it if he made the threat come true. And his brother who was her minister had advised her to go along with his wishes. He had assured her that he had not committed a single act of adultery since all was done in a Christian spirit to help the needy young woman.

Such cases are not helped by any sensible counseling. Some people are asking for human abuse, I have found. I made the woman promise to see a good Christian lawyer. She was using her husband's attorney, by the minister's advice, to save money.

An extreme case? Unfortunately, not in some legalistic churches. My great concern is that one extreme breeds the opposite extreme. A pendulum swings wildly until it can balance in the middle. Satan will try to keep the Christians unbalanced on one side or the other. Jesus stays in the middle.

As Betty prepared her freedom messages she asked me to agree with her in a special prayer request. "I need a practical formula and explanation of what personal freedom in Christ is," she said.

It took us many hours of meditation and searching but by the time she faced the audience she had it in a neat workable package. "Freedom in Christ is a gift, purchased on Calvary, whereby you and Jesus *alone* assume the responsibility for every decision of your life."

I will never forget the breathless hush that fell over the audience as the great truth of this statement began to sink in.

* * * * * * * *

Jesus and you, Jesus and I, that is also the great difference between being alone and being lonely. When we are without human companionship we are alone. No human being can fill another person's loneliness. I learned this from my own experience and in many counseling sessions.

"I feel so lonely because my husband does not understand me," one woman confides.

"The reason I am so lonely is that I am not married," another lady tells me.

"We are the most lonely parents since our son has refused to go to church with us anymore," a father says with tears in his eyes.

"Oh, Hansi, if we only had a child, our happiness

would be perfect," a childless couple assures me.

Why do we humans think that the grass is always greener on the other side?

The Lord Jesus is the only one who can fill human loneliness. Every human being carries that "God-shaped vacuum," as Pascal called it, within himself. The Creator reserved that place for Himself alone. As long as we try to fill it with something or someone else, we must fail. That is so often the reason why homes break up. We demand of each other what only God can give. No other human being can be our life's fulfillment, even if that person wants to. Most of the time it scares a lover when he or she is expected to be responsible for the happiness of the beloved. Smothering is not a sign of love but is born out of fear of freedom. Lonely persons often end up alone because they demand too much from others.

The three messages we recorded about being alone have been among our big tape sellers, together with Betty's tapes on the book of Galatians, Paul's freedom cry.

On our fall tour a nice looking lady had purchased my tapes and came back the next day to thank me. "I think I can handle my mother now," she said and wiped her eyes. "Your tapes helped so much."

"What in particular was helpful?" I asked her.

"You said people cannot become old without becoming bitter or cynical and fed-up with life unless they know the Lord. Everybody's life carries too many rejections, disappointments and shattered dreams to stay sweet and optimistic to the end. You see, my mother is not a Christian. She will not even listen when I try to talk to her about the Lord. The last few years have been so difficult. She has changed so much. Now I understand...."

I encouraged the dear woman to keep loving her mother, pray for her and wait upon the Lord. He obviously was at work in her mother's heart or she would not be so antagonistic to the gospel. Harsh opposition can hurt a Christian's soul painfully, but it is a more encouraging sign than complete indifference.

A lonely Christian has to settle his or her relationship to God first. I found this out in my own life. "But I need someone with skin on," a little boy said to his daddy when he was admonished to trust God during a thunderstorm one night.

I believe that God made us in a way that we need another person's skin to touch or a lap or shoulder on which to lay a heavy head. God said right in the beginning that it was not good for His children to be alone. I am deeply convinced that Jesus can find fulfilling companionship for every one of us, if we let Him.

We need to learn to wait upon Him for everything. But it is crucial in the abundant life of a committed Christian to let God do the selecting of a mate, a friend, a partner, or any other person who steps into our lives.

I have said to my children and to impatient young people who wondered if they would miss the bliss of marriage or parenthood: There is one thing worse than being alone and that is when you have to live with the wrong person twenty-four hours a day.

I remember the time when I walked into the pleasant home of a longtime Christian friend whose husband had just died. It was before my months of extensive travel and I had stood by her during his slow and most painful death. He was a Christian too. He had been her third husband. She told me that the silent house drove her up the walls.

"Couldn't you find another widow or lonely woman to share your cozy home with?" I suggested.

She frowned and said, "I don't think like you do. I need and want a man, and I have told the Lord so."

Of course, she did find another man and got married again. He wasn't a Christian but he was so nice to her. I saw her just recently and she is going through a devastating divorce. The "nice" guy had a most cruel streak of temper which he never displayed while they dated.

She is alone again. I wonder if she is angry with God.

God believes in companionship. He made us and He knows what we need better than we do. Sometimes we delay His provisions for us by running ahead or lagging behind because we are afraid of getting hurt again.

Even the Lord Jesus had His inner circle of friends while He walked the earth. He sent His disciples out by twos to preach His new gospel, never alone. Jesus honored the institution of marriage by performing His first miracle for a dear young couple whose new beginning could have been marred by the shameful exposure of their poverty.

Jesus will never leave us alone, He said so! He knows how terrible it is to be alone. Even God did not know the depth of loneliness until the hour of Calvary. Jesus and the Father had been together always from eternity to the days when the Word became flesh.

Our Lord in human form treasured human friendship but He did not depend on it. "You will all leave Me alone and flee," He said just before Calvary, "but My Father is always with Me."

But the moment came when He found Himself separated from the Father by the sins of the human race. "My God, My God, why hast Thou forsaken Me?" the dying Son of God cried into the lone darkness around the cross. It is the only time in Biblical record that Jesus did not call Him Father, but God. *El* is the name of God's attribute of greatest mercy. And in the moment of utter loneliness Jesus still said, "*My* God!" Our Savior died alone so that we will never have to be alone again.

The cross did not kill Him. The spear of the Roman soldier found an already dead body. My Savior died of a broken heart, crushed by the depth of loneliness that no other human being has ever experienced before or since His death. No one has ever tasted the eternities of perfect togetherness with the Father-God as the Son has. He laid it down, He even risked the loss of it, and He knew it when He pleaded, "Give Me back the glory that I had with You" (John 17:5).

The Father suffered with his Son. We sometimes forget it. If there is one thing harder than to suffer yourself, it is to watch your child in agony, while you stand helplessly by. The Father could have helped His dying Son. While Jesus died on one side of the sin-gulf between heaven and earth, the God of justice and mercy stood on the other side, hearing His beloved Son calling, and turned His back.

Shall we ever be able to comprehend the love of our heavenly Father who gave everything He had to give to save us from eternal loss and separation? Would a God whose Father's heart broke when He watched His only Son's utter abandonment ever send the same despair and loneliness to those who accepted His Son's payment?

A risen Jesus remembered the horrible bitterness of separation when He said as one of His last parting words to the frightened disciples, "I will *never* leave you... I will be with you always." He remembers today and is near to comfort and fill anybody's empty life, if we let Him!

He will also provide human companionship in His perfect time!

* * * * * * * *

We celebrated the best Christmas of my life a week ago. I should have felt alone in the little condominium in Hawaii where we are staying right now. Yes, over in Hawaii a mother can miss her children and I did! Christmas is family time and floods of memories tug and open the door to deep longings. Betty couldn't have kept the pains away either — but the Lord did! He was so near and real.

I had seen all of my children at Thanksgiving at a family reunion at Tina's place. This oldest daughter of mine is a marvelous hostess and we had a perfect time. She made Betty and me feel at home and most welcome. Cathy introduced her fiance to everybody and we obviously will have another wedding in the making. All five of my children live far apart and across the whole continent. So it works out better if each couple can spend Christmas according to their individual tastes and demands. The Lord provided a way to send Betty and me for a rest to my favorite vacation spot: the Big Island of Hawaii. And we needed to get away, we both get so "peopled out"!

We did not put up a Christmas tree. We did not bring any Christmas decorations either. They are all safely packed away in our garage in California. Betty and I love to overdecorate at Christmas. When we are home we usually begin to unpack shortly after Thanksgiving and we act like children. I am so glad we agree that Christmas is a time to be sentimental, "squishy," silly and too much decoration is in good taste during the Christmas season.

Our little impersonal rental unit showed no physical evidence of any celebration — it was all happening in my heart. What peace and light, what music and rejoicing I felt! Why? Because the Lord gave me the desire of my heart and reassured me again about my beloved America and the American people!

While Betty and I served our US troops in Adana in the south of Turkey we had found an isolated village filled with refugees who had to flee war, hunger and persecution. The place they came from was known as Chaldea in Bible times. These people come from a long line of ancestors who had accepted Christianity in a most hostile environment and when the families fled to Turkey they discovered that not much had changed for the better.

The Turkish government might not give the same importance to Moslem beliefs as the leadership in Iran or Iraq but they still hold the same hostility toward non-Moslems as their cruel ancestors did.

The Turks simply don't care if these people live or die and they do *not* permit Christian organizations to come in and help, either.

Children in rags and hopelessness — and I knew we had to find a way to let them know about a caring

Christ. So far they have paid for tenaciously clinging to their ancient Christian worship form only with suffering, pitiful poverty and rejection.

The head chaplain of the nearby US base and I laid plans. We would send needed clothing, shoes, blankets, toys and enough money for a Christmas party. It would be the first these 800 Chaldean refugees ever had!

I don't know if the colonel believed me. We came back last May and went to work on it. I needed board approval and other legal permission. In our September newsletter I poured out my heart to our mailing constituency all over America. I asked for *good* clothing, shoes, baby stuff, toys, etc.

"Don't expect too much" I was warned. "The American people have changed. We are just pulling out of a deep recession, people are still out of work."

I fought my fears, wondering if our "Sonshine project" would result in another big crisis within my soul. If the American people did not respond as I believed they would, I had to change my positive message about America, even this fall!

Thank God, I did not have to change my message. Americans have *not* changed. They would still rather help than hurt. And we have physical proof — five tons of it!

While Betty and I finished our long fall tour, the parcels poured in and our dedicated staff and volunteers worked overtime, sorted, repacked, sealed and shipped. They did not complain, they worked and lifted and rejoiced with us.

All of the air-lifted parcels arrived before Christmas, I read the reports before we left for Hawaii. One letter assured me that the Protestant and Catholic women of our base had things all under control for a Christmas party for the Mersin children. Every child would receive a gift and they would serve a festive meal for everybody.

I have been walking on clouds ever since. All Betty and I had this Christmas was a little tape player and some Christmas tapes. Betty and I didn't even exchange gifts. But I had one of the most wonderful gifts the Lord ever gave me. I pictured the Mersin children celebrating the first Christmas of their lives!

With it came great healing to my own memory. I never had Christmas as a child. Whenever I try to remember I see a little, very lonely girl standing behind an ice-covered window in a small cottage. It is evening and the child has blown her warm breath against the glass to be able to see out. She watches the windows of the neighbors' houses glow in the darkness and she can even see candles flicker on their Christmas trees. Her own house is dark, without candles, no evergreen tree, or even the smallest gift. It was not only poverty, but religious fervor that kept my childhood so destitute. My foster father hated sin and the Catholics. Of the two, the latter was the greater evil. He was able to rationalize the first for himself.

We sang Christmas songs in my one-room elementary school that taught all eight grades. Singing was one of our scheduled subjects. We did it as a combined student group. I wasn't allowed to sing these songs around my foster father. Christmas and the songs were a Catholic invention, he growled, and nobody knew the date of Christ's birth for sure. The songs talked much about *Freude* (joy). I puzzled over it from first grade on. I dreaded that time of the year for many reasons. It was a time of half-frozen toes, long bitter cold nights, monotonous meals, no flowers or birds.

I promised myself as a small girl that I would always have Christmas for my children if I ever had any, or for any other kid that needed it.

I started my own family amidst great poverty as a refugee after World War II, but the Lord always provided something special for Christmas. We always had a little tree, a few candles, and some simple gifts. It was a must for me to "feel" the Christmas spirit.

The little lonely girl in the cottage needed half a century to learn a great truth about the true spirit of

Christmas. A missing Christmas tree neither makes
nor takes away Christmas. Christmas is an attitude, it
is something we must carry within us the whole year.
Freude (joy) comes from sharing and giving, not just
from a little candle.

I shall never forget this Christmas Eve or Betty's and
my celebration of New Year's Eve either!

Christmas Eve became another "silent and holy
night" for us. We drove up to one of our favorite scenic
views high above the ocean and watched a dramatic
sunset. I have learned something for my new photo-
graphy hobby and my final sunset years here on this
earth. Beautiful sunsets need dark clouds before they
can be brilliant and sublime. We don't even reach for
our cameras otherwise. People don't stop around here to
watch an "ordinary" cloudless sunset, though it is
pretty to look at the sun vanishing into the sea. Clouds
magnify the colorful glory of the sinking sun. Life's
difficulties and unanswered questions turn our eyes to
the "Son" who sheds light and hope on our dark mist of
life, and it begins to glow, in His love.

We drove back in the fast-falling night of the tropics.
A star shimmered brightly in the fading sky.

We watched another incredible sunset last night. It
seemed like heaven had lifted a veil and we glimpsed for
a moment into God's unearthly glory.

Betty and I sat enraptured and in utter silence. I
always feel a great longing to hold on to such beauty. It
vanishes so fast.

"Lord," I said in my heart, "if this is a picture of the
glory to come at death, why should God's children
worry and be afraid to come home to You? What will it
be to walk into a never ending sunset and become part
of it? I do not know your plans for us but living or dying,
I am yours.

"I do not know what the future holds, but I know who
holds the future. Please hold me very close and take me
safely home. And, please, don't vanish on me like this
beauty does, I need You, precious Husband and Lord. I

need You every moment of every day. As for this new year, dear Jesus, would You please reveal Yourself *more* to me? How I long to see more of Your glory!"

"Simply trusting every day,
  Trusting through a stormy way;
Even when my faith is small,
  Trusting Jesus, that is all.

Brightly doth His Spirit shine
  Into this poor heart of mine;
While He leads I cannot fall;
  Trusting Jesus, that is all.

Singing if my way is clear;
  Praying if the path be drear;
If in danger, for Him call;
  Trusting Jesus, that is all.

Trusting Him while life shall last,
  Trusting Him till earth be past;
Till within the jasper wall:
  Trusting Jesus, that is all.

Refrain:

Trusting as the moments fly,
  Trusting as the days go by;
Trusting Him whate'er befall,
  Trusting Jesus, that is all."

Edgar P. Stites (1836-1921)

Afterglow

If sunsets are my favorite time of the day, I cherish one part of it most: the afterglow.

In the tropics, the sun sets and the colors vanish but after a time, while dusk and semidarkness dimly cover the land, the clouds begin to glow again. They call it the afterglow and I love its soft beauty the most. It can also linger for a very long time. Sometimes the tropic night has turned already pitchdark and some cloud rims are still shining in a tender shimmer of light.

To me it's God's reassurance that there will *always* be a new day coming.

* * * * * * * *

More than two years ago the Lord nudged me to lay this journal aside. I thought it was finished and we would get the book published. I interpret the Lord's guidance so often as I perceive it best. Most of the time I guess wrong!

The book didn't go into preparation for printing, it just was filed away.

I started a new journal, written with my heart blood*. The last two years have been filled with struggles I never anticipated. We fought with illnesses and hell itself. We sat often in utter darkness and I wondered what Jesus would do next with us. I could not even guess anymore.

Was Betty dying? It looked like it as I watched the little lady slowly but steadily fade away.

"Lord," I would plead, "she doesn't have to be

* See *Better Is Not Enough* booklet, available at Hansi Ministries. Also three tapes: *God's Methods of Healing.*

another Jonathan and leave me so soon? What will happen if You take her home? I need her for research, as a prayer partner and for human companionship. I simply cannot let her go."

Jesus did not give me any earthly reassurance and He did not reveal any "happy endings." "Trust Me," He would say most of the time as I stormed into His presence.

I took Betty to Hawaii. It all started after we had returned from a long, hard but most successful tour all over Europe to serve our US bases. We knew we had "killed ourselves" and were proud of it. We were also sure that the Lord was pleased about it. HE WAS NOT! We both had pushed our aging bodies over the limit and both of us came down with a devastating flu bug we caught in Europe.

Hawaiian paradise can became a very lonely place when your "Kamerad" can't breath or eat or walk more than a few steps and you feel too weak to take care of her. I got slowly stronger but she was failing more and more.

I didn't watch many sunsets and didn't linger for afterglows, Betty was too sick. She would seem to improve and even be able to fulfill her speaking commitments after we left Hawaii, but everytime we thought she had turned the corner, she would relapse even deeper. Nights became pitchblack, starless eternities and God seemed so far away.

I never had any doubt that He could heal her — even instantly. My feelings of great frustration and helpless anger churned in me. Why didn't God come through as we expected? He seemed so unconcerned with our endless struggles.

Praise God that He held on to us when we couldn't be sure of anything anymore. I also thank Him now that we never lost our communication with the Lord completely. We began to call it our "midnight audiences with God" and we had many.

I had prayed to see Christ's glory and I could see only

darkness. Betty fought for every breath and had to force every bite of food down. She lost weight rapidly and her eyes had no more spark. This was the first time of her long life she had to deal with a life-threatening sickness. Betty had been rather healthy all her life. She definitely had been the healthier, stronger and bouncier of the two of us and we both felt devastated.

One night I cried out loud "Lord, Your word tells us that You love us more than we can love each other. I love Betty, she is my closest friend. If I had Your power, Jesus, I would touch her and heal her instantly. Why *don't* You do it? It's not a matter of our faith, we know that You can do it. Our problem is to understand why You don't do it if You love us as much as the Bible says."

The Lord answered but it wasn't the answer I expected. That night Jesus began to teach us to look for His glory in unexpected places. Where we saw only darkness and the shadows of the valley of death, we could see shimmers of light if we only were willing to look in new directions.

We looked, and the last two years have revealed Christ to us as the healing Saviour, and what a glory we beheld!

Yes, Betty recovered and I did too. Our bodies are not above or fully immune to more sickness. We are still climbing out of our long physical exhaustion.

The Lord did not touch our bodies with an instant healing miracle and by now I understand why. If He had done so we would have only raced back to His work and tried our best to kill ourselves to His honor and glory again. Jesus will *never* encourage us to do so, He loves us too much.

We suffered the consequences of our foolish behavior but He never left us. Every moment of agony became a stepping stone to new insights and toward a better life in the future.

I had to learn another big lesson. We can never "claim" a person, even though God had put us together for His service. "If" she were a Jonathan, I had to "let go." I had to release her to the Lord and trust Him to do what was best for her!

The ultimate healing of God happens everytime a saint walks into the final sunset to glory. I had to trust Him by praying "Thy will be done, You know best if she should stay or come home to be with You, no matter how it would affect the ministry, or my own life. Have Your own way, dear Lord."

By the grace of God I learned to pray that prayer. It seemed harder than almost anything else I had ever done (even to forgive my enemies in my turbulent past).

But as I released my "Jonathan" into God's will and care, He was finally able to show us both some important spiritual laws.

She was not another Jonathan just as I am not David and we don't have to follow their earthly path; the Bible stories are not given to us to foretell our physical hardships nor the time of our death. God had just used the story in the beginning of our friendship to show us His way of knitting souls together. He never knits so tightly that we are allowed to become inseparable. We are still unique individuals who first and foremost belong and relate to Jesus, and each one of us has to learn her own personal lessons.

Betty got a heavenly graduate course of immense proportions! It is very hard to keep our eyes on Jesus when we are sick. Betty had no experience how to deal with pain and panic (and what a panic it is when a body doesn't get enough air!) and the Lord saw fit to use the hardest way possible to teach my friend (it's also very trying to watch such struggles).

"Who is your Lord," Jesus came through to both of us in one of our midnight prayer vigils, "Betty's sickness or I?"

"You are Lord," we said and didn't know *how* to keep our eyes on Him.

It got so desperate one night that I finally cried out: "I can't trust You anymore, Jesus, I hit bottom. I can't even pray anymore. Teach us to trust You completely.

It's too hard a prayer, I can't do it."

"It is well that you have arrived at this point," the Lord spoke clearly.

"You mean you approve of it that I can't trust You anymore?" I asked deeply confused.

"My child," Jesus said gently, "remember that you can do nothing without Me? You can't even trust Me in your own strength. I have to give you the trust and then do it for you. Stop trying so hard and let Me do it."

Betty and I talked about our inability to trust for a long time. It opened a new understanding for her, too. She tortured herself because she couldn't "do" something to make the illness go away. Why couldn't she "see" God's remedy for her problem and consequently solve it?

Jesus showed us that "doing" was not our hindrance, we had tried for too long to do too much.

The Lord has to "do" and also heal, and He will always work first through the spirit, next He restores our soul and with it rebuilds our body.

The first step to healing is our humble recognition and confession that we are through with our own doing and let it sink in that we truly can do nothing without Him. We can't even believe or trust in God unless His grace provides us with the ability.

Our head knew it all along, we even had taught it to audiences, but head knowledge must sink into the heart before it can change our troubled lives.

Next the Lord showed us that our will must be pointed like a compass which shows clear directions.

"What is it that you truly want?" the Lord asked.

"We want to be well to serve You," we confessed, "but You shall set the pace and reveal to us our true motives for anything we do."

"Ask for it," the Lord encouraged us, "Ask and believe before the physical evidence is in. Ask for My love and healing and believe it is at work at all times."

We did ask and do keep on asking. Every morning we now accept His restoring and healing power no matter how we "feel" in body or soul. We trust Him in His strength, and that is the third principle He had to teach us. As true as it is that we can do *nothing* without Him, it is equally true that we can do *all* things through Christ, who strengthens us. It is the other side of the same coin and our will holds the balance to both.

The three-pronged spiritual formula sounds so simple and is so readily preached and taught. We learned the depth of its truth when God seemed silent in the valley of the shadows of death.

I do not think that suffering of any kind makes a person automatically more spiritual, be it illness, poverty or other troubles — it often makes us forget some important spiritual but simple truths.

We got so deeply involved with fighting the deep shadows, we forgot that shadows can only scare us, they cannot hurt us. They are not death itself and we are not subject to it.

Another thing we had forgotten was that our Shepherd had promised His presence in the valley and He also assures us that He is leading us *through* the scary place. We shall always come out into the light on the other side!

Psalm 23 has a new special meaning to both of us. Life itself carries a new glow. We enjoy food, we take time to smell the flowers.

We are both well enough to serve God's people better than we did before. God gave us a deeper compassion and a greater tolerance not only toward each other but for others we work and associate with every day.

Jesus is nearer than ever and I am glad. He is a wonderful Husband!

I don't wonder any longer if the honeymoon is over. If it is, I got something much better and more solid from Him.

I have found out that I can do nothing without Him. But if I truly want to do His will, I can do *all things* through Christ.

I don't know what "all things" mean for the future. I

don't even try to outguess the Lord's leading anymore.

I have no idea how soon or long it will be before either Betty or I will walk into the final sunset. Someday in the afterglow of heaven I shall see His face. He will explain all the "whys" to me and I shall understand all the things I have not known.

One thing I do know for now and until eternity...
I shall never walk alone again.

Surrounded by humans
   yet fully alone
Hopeless despondent
   low heartbroken moan
Seemingly friendless
   life offers no gain
Trying so bravely
   to hide all the pain.

Receive now His comfort
   engulfed by His love
Feel His warm presence
   and pow'r from above.
Know in your heart
   that God's on His throne
And we, His dear children
   walk never alone.

                                      Phebe

Other Books from Hansi Ministries

I Am But a Child in Christ
Follow Me
Learn of Me
God's Word: A Living Rainbow
Rainbow Guide
Better Is Not Enough

Also Available:
Books on Hansi's Life
Books on Our Times
Bible Study Tapes by Maria Anne Hirschmann (Hansi)
Bible Study Tapes by Betty Pershing
Tapes on America, Freedom and Christian Growth

If these books are unavailable at your bookstore, please send order with check to cover retail price, plus $1.00 per book for postage and handling to:

Hansi Ministries
P.O. Box 3009
Fallbrook, CA 92028

Prices subject to change without notice.